Anita Hinson Cauthen

ISBN: 978-1-954614-27-7 (Hard cover)

Edited by: Sheryl Tharpe and Monika Dziamka
Cover Design by: Coleman Tharpe

Published by Warren Publishing
Charlotte, NC
www.warrenpublishing.net
Printed in the United States

I loved everything. We lived in Kershaw, and when we came to Lancaster, a trip to the bakery was a highlight. Mom usually got tea biscuits for Sunday dinner or some other occasion, and I got a gingerbread man or brownie. My husband loved the thumbprint cookies. I tried to make them for him, but I never got it right. He liked the butter cookies. Great memories.

–CAROLYN CLYBURN HARDIN

I have so many good memories of the Lancaster Bakery. When I was a little girl, my mother and I would go to the West Gay Street bakery on Saturdays and get some of the delicious goodies and biscuits. When the bakery moved to Main Street, we still went there a lot. Everything was so good, but my favorite was the tea cookies. When I got to high school, I worked at the bakery on Saturdays and one summer too. Great memories of the Courtney and Hinson families and working with Mrs. Ruth Baker and Mrs. Creola Powell.

–HILDA FAULKENBERRY COOK

I grew up across the street from the Lancaster Bakery on West Gay Street. Often, after an early morning ambulance call, my brother Snooks and I would go to the back door of the bakery and swap six cold Cokes for twelve hot donuts with the cooks. Better than Krispy Kreme!

–HAZEL CAUTHEN

Best Bakery EVER! Great day in the morning! Miss Jeanie Reid used to work there. I'll never forget my birthday cakes from this bakery!!!!
—BRIDGETTE FRAZIER LOWERY

I'm always telling my husband how wonderful their stickies were. Daddy would go early in the morning when they had just come out of the oven. I've searched everywhere for the recipe to no avail.
—ANN YARBOROUGH FOSNACHT

Never had a better donut since. Yes, this was the greatest bakery ever. I have traveled the world, and never have I found a better bakery. Oh, the memories of the great bakery goods bought there.
—JIM KNIGHT

I would go on Saturday afternoon and buy a small birthday cake every week. They would be reduced!! Best Ever.
—JAN RODDEY WESTMORELAND-SIPES

CUSTOMER MEMORIES

Going to the Lancaster Bakery was always a treat for me. Of all of the delicious offerings, the chocolate cookies with white icing inside will forever be the best cookies ever! Over the years I have tried to replicate them, but to no avail! Another very special favorite was the Easter egg cake. It was much larger than the size of an egg … my memory says it was almost as large as a football. It was iced and decorated beautifully. The Easter Bunny put one in my basket for many years!! Another real treat was the iced raisin bread … I could go on and on, but the three I mentioned were by far my favorites. My mother and D.B. Courtney were good friends, and it was always fun to listen to them chat. Childhood memories remind me that I was very fortunate to grow up in Lancaster.

—MERRIO MORTON

When I was in grammar school, my mom took me to the old post office to meet my 4th, 5th, and 6th grade teachers so I could continue going to McDonald Green School. In the afternoon when I returned, I would stop by the bakery and get a dozen tea cookies and eat them on my walk home. I can still taste them, and it has been lots of years since then. What I would give for some now! Loved that place.

—JUDY S. MUNN

This book is dedicated to the past, present, and future small business owners of Lancaster County, South Carolina.

PROLOGUE

My identical twin sister Rita and I entered this world on the evening of October 30, 1949, in Lancaster, South Carolina. Our family's bakery, the Lancaster Bakery, had opened years earlier in March 1940 and continued to serve the local community for over four decades. It was an established, integral part of the town and provided a steady income for the Courtneys, the Hinsons, and their employees. Our household included Rita and me, our older brother Donald (aka Ernie to his friends), my mother, my father, my grandmother, my grandfather, and my uncle. Our eating, sleeping, playing, and working hours centered on the bakery.

Growing up in an extended family with five adults was uncommon in Lancaster in the 1950s. Perhaps even more unusual for many households today, my sister and I shared a bedroom with our older brother Donald until he married. He was seven years older and seemed to resent our very existence during his teen years. Of course, we didn't help the situation. Whenever his girlfriends called to speak to Ernie, Rita and I always told them no one with that name lived in our house!

My memories and many requests for recipes from prior patrons were the motivation for writing this memoir. More than a collection of recipes, it depicts a way of life before the world became so small and perhaps more isolated through technology. My memoir represents a time when people in communities and towns obtained goods and services from their neighbors and friends. It was also a time when smiles mattered and when community was family.

Everything reflects my Southern childhood in Lancaster. So, I have organized my memoir into small sections, based on the seasons and my childhood memories, each with its own tastes, smells, and emotions. Finally, it is a tribute to the Lancaster Bakery and many other small businesses in our community.

This epitaph to my family's bakery business was published in the *Historic Lancaster 2003 Calendar*: "A trip to Lancaster Bakery could cure any sweet tooth, or tempt it to make a repeat visit. The bakery opened its doors on West Gay Street on March 29, 1940. It was later moved to its location at 222 S. Main St. The bakery closed its doors in the early 1980s."

RECIPE CONVERSION PROCESS

Professional bakers measure ingredients in weight (pounds/ounces) using balanced bakers scales instead of volume (cups/tablespoons). They also buy commercial ingredients in bulk from bakery suppliers to produce large quantities of baked goods (i.e., liquid eggs, chocolate fudge base, milk powder, etc.). My converting the bakery's recipes into recipes for use by an individual or a family was a time-consuming process. For the included recipes, I converted large batches of products from ingredients measured by weight into small batches of products with ingredients measured by volume for home baking. The weight measurements are also provided for people who want to use a digital scale for more accurate baking. I highly recommend Escali's PANA Digital Scale.

My other challenge was finding substitutes in today's grocery stores for the commercial ingredients listed in the bakery's recipes. Many of the recipe ingredients include milk powder and lemon juice powder. Professional bakers use these powders because they have a stable shelf life. Instead, you can try substituting liquid milk for the water and lemon juice for the lemon juice powder. My recommended resource for baking supplies is the King Arthur Baking Company (www.kingarthurbaking.com). From this site, I purchased several ingredients, such as the Baker's Special Dry Milk and Lemon Juice Powder. I hope my efforts have been successful!

TABLE OF CONTENTS

Lancaster Bakery, July 6, 1955

LANCASTER: THEN AND NOW

*T*he Lancaster area thrived during the twentieth century with the opening of the Lancaster Cotton Mill by Colonel Leroy Springs in 1896. Located in an area of Lancaster known as Midway, it was known as the world's largest textile plant under one roof. Houses were built in the vicinity to provide homes for the mill workers, and small businesses opened nearby to provide goods and services to the mill workers and their families.

In 1993, international trade regulations changed, and more and more of the textile industry production was exported from the United States. The Lancaster Cotton Mill closed in 2003, forcing many citizens in Lancaster to seek jobs elsewhere in nearby York County, South Carolina, and Charlotte, North Carolina. In the years that followed, both city and county leaders worked hard to promote business in the area. Today the northern Lancaster County panhandle, known as Indian Land, has become a growing economic hub with sprawling residential developments. Indian Land also serves as a business incubator and tax haven for businesses seeking to leave cities in both South Carolina and other states.

E.N. Courtney – Belk's anniversary cake

THE BAKERY FAMILY

*E*rnest Nebraska (E.N.) Courtney, my grandfather whom we grandchildren called Pawpaw, was the first entrepreneur I ever met. Born in Lancaster County in 1888, he lived in a small community called Van Wyck (rhymes with "bike"). There he met and married my grandmother, Lula Starnes Courtney. They raised four children in Van Wyck. During these years, he managed the Van Wyck general store. In the 1930s, he moved his family to help my grandmother's widowed sister, Azilee Hernig, run a bakery in Monroe, North Carolina.

In 1939, my grandfather decided to open his own bakery in Lancaster, about forty miles southwest of Monroe. Even though some told him a bakery would never survive in that area, he proved the naysayers wrong. He worked seven days a week doing what he loved until he succumbed to cancer in 1966. I was at Pawpaw's side when he uttered his last words: "Thank you. Come back to see us." These were the same words that he always said to customers leaving the bakery. After Pawpaw's death, my father, my mother, and my Uncle D.B. (Courtney) inherited the business.

In the February 13, 2009 issue of *The Lancaster News,* the late Mr. W.B. Evans (a local historian) wrote the article "Chicken Biz for the Birds, Bakery." Mr. Evans reminisced about the chicken house in the barn behind his childhood home on Chesterfield Avenue in Lancaster. He reminded everyone about the short supply of sugar and eggs during World War II.

Then Mr. Evans shared how Pawpaw found some extra, much needed eggs for the bakery. My clever grandfather regularly obtained a fresh supply of local eggs from Mr. Evans' mother in exchange for donuts. With much hard work, my grandfather managed to keep the bakery open during all the years of war rationing. Yet my family suffered heartbreak when my grandparents lost their first-born son, Private First Class Ernest N. Courtney, during the Bataan Death March in the Philippines in April 1942.

My grandmother and my mother, Louise Courtney Hinson, were responsible for house cleaning, washing and ironing clothes, raising three children, and putting three meals a day on the table. We children called our grandmother Mawmaw and our mother Mama. In the mid-1950s, my grandmother was diagnosed with a brain tumor. Her subsequent surgery removed too much of her brain matter, and she returned home with no memories, no ability to speak or care for herself. I have only one pre-surgery memory of my grandmother, but it is a happy one: Mawmaw is sitting in her beige recliner, watching Friday night boxing, and sipping on a Schlitz. After rimming the can with salt, she would give me a sip when no one was looking.

Now all of the household duties fell on my mother after Mawmaw's surgery. Mama had to care for my grandmother's daily needs in addition to everything else. Sadly, after a couple of years, my mother was so worn down that the family made the painful decision to admit Mawmaw to the South Carolina State Hospital in Columbia, South Carolina. Regularly my Uncle D.B. would drive Pawpaw, Rita, and me to visit my grandmother. (My parents visited when my father had time off from work.) During those afternoons, we would sit on the hospital grounds and help Mawmaw consume sweets brought from the bakery.

Robert Jackson (Buck) Hinson, Daddy to his children, began his baker's career as an apprentice baker at the Monroe Bakery. There he met, fell in love with, and married my mother. Soon afterward they moved to Lancaster, and he became the lead baker for the Lancaster Bakery.

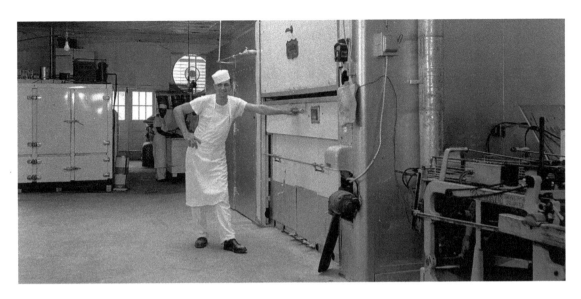

Buck's production area—Lancaster Bakery at the 112 West Gay Street location

All employees at the bakery worked long hours. The bakery opened for business from 6:00 a.m. until 6:00 p.m. on Monday through Saturday. Routinely my father arrived several hours before his staff and began his workday at 2:00 a.m. on Monday through Friday. His twelve-hour shifts ended at 2:00 p.m. However, on Fridays, he also worked from 9:00 p.m. until Saturday morning at 8:00. He clearly recognized that he and his staff were responsible for producing the many different confections that our community craved.

Then at 4:30 a.m. on Monday through Saturday, my grandfather arrived to prepare the racks of pastries and donuts for the storefront. Regardless of the time of year, he would make weekly batches of ice cream for customers. Carefully he measured the flavorings of vanilla, chocolate, cherry, butter pecan, and lemon; he next added sugar and milk; and then he started the automated ice cream churn. While the most popular flavors were lemon and butter pecan, my favorite was chocolate. The three-gallon containers of ice cream were stored in the storefront's subzero freezer, from which an employee with a strong arm scooped the ice cream into the cones. Naturally the bakery sold more ice cream in the hot, humid summers.

The bakery remained quite busy from early on Friday until Saturday closing. In fact, Friday morning was the busiest day after the third shift at the textile mill ended. My Uncle D.B. cashed paychecks for workers and then sold cakes and pies to them for their weekend dinners. Thanks to my father's late-night work on Fridays, the bakery always had a sufficient number of cakes and pies available to customers on Saturday.

D.B. Courtney helping a customer at the 112 West Gay Street location

Yet what about the items unsold by Saturday's closing? Unlike today, preservatives weren't used in baked goods to maintain freshness. So, every Sunday after church, my grandfather opened the bakery and sold the week's remaining products at one-half price. Even Rita and I helped on many Sunday afternoons by assembling stacks and stacks of boxes for the bakery to be ready for the next week's sales of cakes, pies, pastries, and cookies.

Bakers and sales staff, 1955: Buck Hinson, first on left;
Creola Powell, third from left; Mary Alice Mullis, fourth from left;
D.B. Courtney, fifth from left; E.N. Courtney, sixth from left

In the mid-1960s when Belk's Department Store took over the 112 West Gay Street location, the Lancaster Bakery moved to a renovated movie theater at 222 South Main Street. This new location had a coffee bar with stools and a few tables and chairs. Now the bakery welcomed office workers with the aromas of freshly brewed coffee, sweets, and sausage and ham biscuits. The upstairs balcony was leased for privately catered events, and it was also used for meetings of the local Weight Watchers' chapter. Not surprisingly, the bakery tempted many chapter members!

Lancaster Bakery at the 222 South Main Street location. The Lancaster Bakery sign is currently on display in The Shops on Main, an antique mall at 212 South Main Street.

During the mid-1960s, my family also grew the business by opening a bakery in the Westgate Shopping Center on Meeting Street in Lancaster and by purchasing Betty's Cake Box in nearby Rock Hill. Within two years, both of these locations were closed because of insufficient foot traffic to cover the costs.

My brother Donald and I chose not to continue the business as family members grew old and sick and died. Some days I question if I made the right decision. Still, I remain thankful to have the recipes on yellowed index cards, some black and white photos, and many wonderful memories of my family and the Lancaster Bakery.

ALL SEASONS

Our family lived in a one-story white clapboard house at 310 West Gay Street. The house had a large wrap-around porch where family and neighbors would gather on late afternoons. Behind the house was a large two-story building that housed two one-car garages, a storage area for bakery supplies, and a one-bedroom upstairs apartment that provided rental income. Our childhood experiences were within a two-block walking distance: Central Elementary School; Lancaster High School; the Lancaster County Library; offices of Doctors Harris, Smith, Horton, and Sims; 5 and 10 Cent stores; Taylor's Grocery; Mackey's Drugstore; the Lancaster Cafe; Mr. Flack's store; the First United Methodist Church; movie theaters; and, of course, the Lancaster Bakery.

During school holidays, summer months, and weekends, Rita and I helped prepare the baked goods for sale. After we learned to add and count back change, we were allowed to work in sales. Often on early, dark mornings, Rita, my grandfather, and I walked the one block from home to the bakery. On especially hard workdays before lunch time, my grandfather would give both my sister and me a nickel to spend. Then we had to decide on comics or candy at Mackey's Drugstore on the corner of Gay and Main Streets or toys at Cox's or Mack's local 5 and 10 Cent stores. Big decisions for us youngsters at the time!

At thirteen, Donald began working the early morning shift at 4:30. His primary duties were putting cooled pastries on trays, wrapping rolls, and delivering pies and cakes to the Lancaster Cafe, Tiny Town Restaurant, and other places before his school day. Later in high school when he became a player on the Lancaster Hurricane basketball team, late-night games cut into his sleep time prior to work. Somehow Donald persevered and continued working hard, sometimes for long hours. During high school summer breaks, he cooked donuts and assumed additional baker duties. Once in 1959, he missed his workday but had a good excuse. He had totaled his 1955 Bel Air, rounding a dead man's curve on Riverside Road late at night but was able to walk away and get a ride home. Once there, he awoke our grandfather and explained why he would not be going to work that morning!

Most Saturdays after lunch, Rita and I walked from our home to Midway to watch matinees at the Hyatt Movie Theater. Mama would give each of us twenty-five cents, which covered our admission, a drink, and popcorn or candy to last us through the afternoon. Usually we watched feature films once, but sometimes we sat through movies twice! My sister and I were fond of Elvis Presley and Pat Boone movies.

Another local business we liked to visit in Midway was Dabney's Music Store. Mrs. Dabney sold popular sheet music, 78 rpm albums, and 45 rpm singles. In addition, she would often play the latest hit singles for customers. Thanks to Uncle D.B., Rita and I were quite familiar with all the popular vocalists like Della Reese, Fats Domino, Chubby Checker, and Frankie Valli and the Four Seasons, so we were always happy to hear the new songs. We were even happier when Uncle D.B. had an afternoon off from work and could join us.

Actually, music provided much pleasure to our entire family on many evenings or weekend afternoons. When home, Uncle D.B. found time to play both popular songs and hymns from the piano sheet music he had bought from Dabney's. Rita and I would sit on either side of him on the piano bench and sing. Some of our favorite songs were "Green Door," "Tammy," "Singing the Blues," "Since I Met You Baby," "In the Garden," and "How

Great Thou Art." Daddy, who sang baritone, liked to join in on hymns. To everyone's delight and surprise, Rita sat at the piano after the sing-alongs and played the songs by ear without sheet music. That is how we discovered that Rita had an ability to hear music once and reproduce it on any musical instrument. In addition to the piano, she played an accordion, a violin, and a harmonica.

Rita's musical abilities were a blessing, but she also lived with a neurological disorder known as epilepsy. Most of her seizures were known as petit mal. During this type of seizure, Rita had a blank stare and made humming noises. Her seizures typically lasted under a minute and could occur several times a day. On several occasions she had the grand mal seizure where she convulsed and lost consciousness. These convulsions were terrifying to witness, and she required a doctor visit.

Rita performing in a local talent show in 1958

Over the years, my parents took Rita to several medical centers, but no effective medication was available then to control her seizures. In 1958, when Rita and I were nine years old, doctors at the Medical University of South Carolina, located in Charleston, contacted my parents to inform them that the university was conducting research on epilepsy. In particular, the doctors questioned why one twin had epilepsy and the other twin did not. Daddy drove Mama, Rita, and me to Charleston for the tests. The doctors glued patches connected to wires to our scalps. The wires were connected to an electroencephalogram (EEG), a test to measure electrical activity in the brain. While I clearly remember the EEG tests, I specifically recall how long it took Mama to remove the glue from our hair. For decades, no one discussed the outcome of the tests. Then in 1981 when Mama was dying from lung cancer, she called me over to her bedside and told me the results of the EEG tests: I also should have suffered from epilepsy.

During our elementary school years, Rita attended classes even though her seizures caused occasional disruptions. However, she did not attend the public middle and high schools because no programs were yet offered for special-needs children. For several years, my parents hired a retired teacher to come to the house to tutor Rita. For the rest of her life, she worked at the Lancaster Bakery. Rita led a lonely life with minimal opportunities to enlarge her social circle.

RECIPES

*C*ertain goods were available every day of the year. This section includes the most remembered best sellers.

Butter Cookies

Yield: Approximately 4 ½ dozen cookies.

Ingredients:

1 ½ cups (6 oz.) confectioners' sugar
1 tsp. salt
⅓ cup (1.6 oz.) nonfat milk powder
1 ¾ cups (12.6 oz.) shortening
1 tsp. vanilla extract
1 tsp. butter extract
⅛ tsp. yellow food coloring
2 eggs
3 oz. water
4 cups (18.9 oz.) cake flour

Directions:

1. Preheat oven to 350^0 F.
2. Have all ingredients at room temperature.
3. Cream lightly the confectioners' sugar, salt, milk powder, shortening, vanilla extract, butter extract, and yellow food coloring on low speed.
4. Add the eggs slowly, one at a time, and mix on low speed until blended.
5. Add the water slowly and mix on low speed until incorporated.
6. Sift in the flour and mix until just combined.

7. Using a pastry bag fitted with a 1 M (½-inch) star tube, deposit quarter-size dough 2 inches apart on a parchment-lined baking sheet. (Test with a little dough. If the dough is too hard to pipe, mix a little water in the remaining dough.)

8. Make a small indentation in the center of each cookie, and add half of a candied cherry or a dollop of cherry jam.

9. Place the baking sheet in the refrigerator for 20–30 minutes to help prevent the cookies from spreading while baking.

10. Place the baking sheet in the oven and bake the cookies for 12–15 minutes or until edges and bottoms are slightly golden.

11. Move the baking sheet to a wire rack to cool for 10 minutes. Slide the parchment onto a wire rack to finish cooling.

Chocolate Sandwich Cookies

Yield: Approximately 2 ½ to 3 dozen sandwich cookies.

Ingredients:

For Cookies:
2 ½ cups (18.2 oz.) granulated sugar
1 ¼ cups (3.6 oz.) cocoa powder
1 ½ cups (10.9 oz.) lard
4 eggs
⅓ cup (3.6 oz.) molasses
1 tsp. vanilla and butter flavoring
  (may just use 1 tsp. of vanilla extract)
3 ⅓ cups (16.4 oz.) cake flour

For Buttercream Icing:
7 ¼ cups (30 oz.) confectioners' sugar
½ cup ice water
⅔ tsp. vanilla extract
1 ¼ cups (8 oz.) shortening
⅓ cup (1.5 oz.) cake flour
1 tsp. salt

Directions:

1. Preheat oven to 375° F.
2. Have all the ingredients at room temperature.
3. Whisk together the granulated sugar and cocoa.
4. Add the lard and mix on low speed until creamed lightly.
5. Add the eggs one at a time and blend on low speed.
6. Add the molasses and the vanilla and butter flavoring (or just the vanilla flavoring) and blend on low speed.
7. Sift in the flour and mix on low until just combined.
8. Using a small cookie scoop (No. 50, 1.25 Tbs.), drop the dough 2 inches apart on a parchment-lined baking sheet.
9. Place the baking sheet in the oven and bake the cookies for 8–9 minutes until edges begin to crisp.
10. Move the baking sheet to a wire rack to cool for 10 minutes. Slide the parchment onto a wire rack to finish cooling prior to icing.

Mixing Buttercream Icing:

1. Mix the sugar, water, and vanilla extract.
2. Add a small amount of shortening.
3. Mix until all lumps are out.
4. Add the balance of shortening.
5. Add the flour and salt.
6. Mix on 2nd speed for 12 minutes or until creamy consistency.
7. Spoon the icing into a pastry bag fitted with a plain tube. *Tip: Line a large glass with the pastry bag and overlap the top of the glass. Spoon the mixture into the lined glass.*
8. Pipe the icing onto the flat side on one cookie and top with another cookie.

Oatmeal Cookies

Yield: Approximately 4 dozen cookies.

Ingredients:

2 ⅓ cups (16.5 oz.) granulated sugar
⅓ tsp. salt
1 ¼ cups (9.2 oz.) shortening
1 ⅔ tsp. baking soda
¼ tsp. lemon extract
1 tsp. ground cinnamon
½ cup (1.6 oz.) vanilla pound cake or vanilla Bundt cake, crumbled
3 eggs
2 ½ cups (12.4 oz.) cake flour
3 ½ cups (6.2 oz.) rolled oats
⅔ cup (3.9 oz.) raisins

Directions:

1. Preheat oven to 375⁰ F.
2. Have all ingredients at room temperature.
3. Cover the raisins in cold water and let them soak for 10–15 minutes.
4. Drain the water and grind the raisins using a hand-cranked food grinder or a food processor.
5. Cream the granulated sugar, salt, shortening, baking soda, lemon extract, cinnamon, and cake crumbs on low speed for about 3 minutes.
6. Add the eggs one at a time while mixing on low speed.
7. In a separate bowl, blend the cake flour, oats, and ground raisins.
8. Add the oats, cake flour, and ground raisins to the creamed mixture and mix until smooth.
9. Using a No 40 (1.75 Tbs.) cookie scoop, scoop the cookies and place 2 inches apart on a parchment-lined baking sheet.
10. Place the baking sheet in the oven and bake the cookies for 8–10 minutes.
11. Move the baking sheet to a wire rack to cool for 15 minutes. Slide parchment onto a wire rack to finish cooling.

Sweet Dough for Pastries

Ingredients:

4 tsp. instant yeast
⅔ cup (4.8 oz.) granulated sugar
1 ¾ tsp. salt
⅓ cup (1.6 oz.) nonfat milk powder
2 ½ tsp. (.40 oz.) baking powder
4 ⅓ cups (20.8 oz.) bread flour
1 ⅓ cups (6.4 oz.) cake flour
⅔ cup (4.8 oz.) shortening
2 eggs
1 ⅔ cups cold water
4 sticks (16 oz.) unsalted butter

Directions:

1. In a mixing bowl, whisk the instant yeast, granulated sugar, salt, powdered milk, baking powder, bread flour, and cake flour.
2. Add the shortening to the whisked ingredients, and work the shortening in with your fingers or a pastry blender until there are no large lumps.
3. Add 1 ⅔ cups cold water and eggs.
4. Mix on medium speed with paddle attachment until ingredients are combined. Then switch to a dough hook and kneed about 3 minutes. (The dough will be sticky.)
5. Dust the dough lightly with flour, wrap the dough in plastic wrap, and rest the dough on the countertop while you prepare the butter.

6. Cut each stick of butter in half lengthwise.
7. Place four pieces of the butter on a piece of plastic wrap, dust with small amount of flour, and cover with another piece of plastic wrap.
8. Pound lightly and roll the butter into about a 6 x 9 inch rectangle. Repeat this procedure with the remaining four pieces of butter.
9. Roll out the dough to about a 12 x 24 inch rectangle.
10. Place one sheet of butter over the center third of the dough (B).
11. Fold the dough without the butter over the center third (C to B).
12. Place the remaining sheet of butter over the folded-over dough (B).
13. Fold the remaining third on top (A to B).

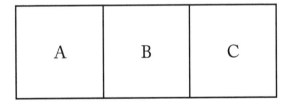

14. Turn the dough 90⁰ so the long side is facing you. Roll the dough into about a 10 x 24 inch rectangle. Fold each side of the dough over the center (C to B and A to B). Fold one side of dough (B) over the other side to make a packet about 6 x 10 inches.

15. Dust the top of the dough with flour.
16. Wrap the dough in plastic wrap and refrigerate for 20 minutes.
17. Remove the dough from the refrigerator, and place the dough on the lightly floured surface.
18. Repeat step 14. Then roll one final time, fold into a packet, and lightly dust with flour.
19. Wrap the dough loosely in plastic wrap, and chill the dough at least 2 hours, or up to 16 hours.

Tip: When you are ready to prepare the pastries for baking, work with half of the dough at a time. Keep the other half in the refrigerator.

Sticky Buns

Yield: Approximately 2 dozen pastries.

Ingredients:

For Honey Topping:
2 cups (16 oz.) brown sugar
4 Tbs. shortening
6 Tbs. honey

Directions:

1. Prepare the Sweet Dough for Pastries *(see page 17)*.
2. Roll out the dough into a rectangle to about ¼ inch thick.
3. Roll the dough up like a jelly roll.
4. Slice the dough into 1 inch pieces.
5. Cut each piece in half, almost through.
6. Grease a baking sheet.
7. Spread half of the honey topping evenly on the baking sheet.
8. Open the dough pieces and press onto the baking sheet, 2 inches apart.
9. Using your fingers, shape each piece into 2 inch by 4 inch figure-eight rectangles.
10. Pour or brush the remaining honey topping over the top and sides of the dough.
11. Cover the dough with greased plastic wrap and set in a warm place (about 75 ^{0} F) until the dough has risen slightly in size and the dough springs back slowly when lightly touched (about an hour to an hour and a half).
12. Place the baking sheet in 375^0 F preheated oven for about 18-25 minutes or until the stickies are golden brown.
13. Remove the baking sheet from the oven and flip the stickies, top-side down, onto racks to cool.

Mixing Honey Toping:

1. Place the brown sugar, shortening, and honey in a saucepan.
2. Heat and stir over medium heat until the sugar is dissolved.

Danish Pastry

Yield: Approximately 3 dozen pastries.

Ingredients:

For Streusel Topping:

3 ⅓ cups (16 oz.) bread flour
1 ¼ cups (8 oz.) granulated sugar
1 cup (6.7 oz.) shortening
Pinch of salt
1 egg
1 tsp. vanilla extract
Egg wash: 1 egg beaten with 1 Tbs. water or milk
Optional: ⅛ tsp. yellow food coloring
Optional: ¼ cup (1 oz.) chopped nuts

For Glaze:

1 ½ cups confectioners' sugar
3 Tbs. water

Directions:

1. Prepare the Sweet Dough for Pastries *(see page 17).*
2. Roll out the dough into a rectangle to about ¼ inch thick and 8 inches wide.
3. Cut the dough into 1-inch by 8-inch strips.
4. Gently lift the dough and twist the opposite ends in opposing directions into a loose rope.
5. Spiral the rope around itself to form a loose circle/spiral and tuck the end under the dough.
6. Place the dough 2 inches apart onto a baking sheet lined with parchment paper.
7. Cover the dough with a towel and set in a warm place (about 75⁰ F) until the dough has risen slightly in size and the dough springs back slowly when lightly touched (about an hour to an hour and a half).
8. Brush the tops of the dough with egg wash.
9. Spoon a thick layer of the streusel over the top of the dough.
10. Place the baking sheet in 375⁰ F preheated oven for about 15–18 minutes or until the pastries are golden brown.
11. Remove the baking sheet from the oven and drizzle the glaze over the top of the pastries.

Mixing Streusel:

1. Combine the bread flour, sugar, shortening, and salt in a bowl. Rub mixture well until crumbly.
2. Stir in lightly beaten egg and vanilla. *Optional: Add yellow food coloring.*
3. Mix on low speed until combined.

Mixing Glaze:

1. Place 1 ½ cups of confectioners' sugar into a mixing bowl.
2. Add water slowly while stirring until glaze is thin enough to drizzle from a spoon. *Optional: Stir ¼ cup of chopped nuts in the glaze.*

Sweet Buns

Yield: Approximately 3 dozen pastries.

Ingredients:

For Bun Icing:
2 cups (16 oz.) brown sugar
1 ¼ cups (8 oz.) shortening
¼ tsp. salt
½ tsp. vanilla extract
3 Tbs. honey
¼ cup water

Egg wash:
1 egg beaten with 1 Tbs. water or milk
Optional: Jam for filling

Directions:

1. Prepare the Sweet Dough for Pastries (*see page 17*).
2. Scale (weigh) the dough into 1 ½ ounce pieces or scoop the dough using a No. 20 (3 Tbs.) cookie scoop.
3. Roll the dough into flattened balls, about 3 inches in diameter.
4. Place the dough 2 inches apart onto a baking sheet lined with parchment paper.
5. Cover the dough with a towel and set in a warm place (about 75⁰ F) until the dough has risen slightly in size and the dough springs back slowly when lightly touched (about an hour to an hour and a half).
6. Brush the tops of the dough with egg wash. *Optional: Using your fingers, make a 1 ½ inch wide indentation in the center of each bun. Fill the indentation with desired jam filling.*
7. Place the baking sheet in 375⁰ F preheated oven for about 10–15 minutes or until the buns are golden brown.

Mixing Icing:

1. Cream the brown sugar, shortening, salt, and vanilla extract.
2. Mix in the honey.
3. Mix in water until you achieve the desired consistency.
4. Ice the warm pastries with the bun spread.

Bear Claws

Yield: Approximately 2 dozen pastries.

Ingredients:

For Almond Filling:
8 oz. almond paste, broken into
   small pieces
1 ¼ cups (8 oz.) granulated sugar
1 cup (7 oz.) shortening
⅓ cup cake flour
1 egg
½ cup (2 oz.) sliced almonds

Or

For Date Filling:
16 oz. dates, pitted
½ cup granulated sugar
1 cup (8 oz.) water
Egg wash: 1 egg beaten with 1 Tbs.
water or milk

Directions:

1. Prepare the Sweet Dough for Pastries *(see page 17)*.
2. Roll the dough into a rectangle ¼ inch thick.
3. Spread the almond filling or the cooled date filling over the dough.
4. Roll up the dough like a jelly roll.
5. Cut the dough into 4-inch pieces.
6. Flatten the dough slightly and cut ½ inch slits in the edge of the dough.
7. Place the pieces of dough on a parchment-lined baking sheet 2 inches apart.
8. Bend the dough into a curve.
9. Cover the dough with a towel and set in a warm place (about 75⁰ F) until the dough has risen slightly in size and the dough springs back slowly when lightly touched (about an hour to an hour and a half).
10. Brush the tops of the dough with egg wash.
11. Sprinkle sliced almonds on top if using the almond filling.
12. Place the baking sheet in a 375⁰ F preheated oven for about 10–15 minutes or until the pastries are golden brown.
Optional: Mix 1 cup of confectioners' sugar with 2 Tbs. of water and drizzle on top of cooled bear claws.

Mixing Almond Filling:

1. Mix together the almond paste and the granulated sugar.
2. Add the shortening and cake flour and blend until smooth.
3. Add the egg and mix until smooth.

Or

Mixing Date Filling:

1. Grind the dates with a hand-held grinder or a food processor.
2. Put the dates, sugar, and water in a saucepan and bring to a boil.
3. Simmer while stirring until the filling is thick and smooth.

Chocolate Eclairs

Yield: Approximately 2 dozen eclairs.

Ingredients:

For Custard Filling:

2 ¼ cups granulated sugar

1 Tbs. margarine

3 ¾ tsp. salt

4 cups water (divided into 3 cups and 1 cup)

1 cup nonfat milk powder

⅔ cup (3 oz.) ClearJel
 (may substitute cornstarch)

3 eggs

For Eclair shells:

2 ½ cups water (divided into 2 cups and ½ cup)

1 ¼ cups (8 oz.) shortening

2 ½ cups (12 oz.) bread flour

12 eggs

1 Tbs. (½ oz.) baking ammonia
 (may substitute baking powder)

For Chocolate Glaze:

⅓ cup water

⅓ cup light corn syrup

1 cup granulated sugar

8 oz. semisweet chocolate, chopped

Directions:

Mixing Custard Filling:

1. Bring the granulated sugar, margarine, salt, 3 cups of water, and milk powder to a boil in a medium saucepan.
2. Dissolve the ClearJel in 1 cup of water and mix in the eggs.
3. Add the dissolved ingredients slowly to the boiling mixture and stir well.
4. Remove from the heat as it thickens.
5. After 10 minutes, press plastic wrap on top of the custard and refrigerate at least 2 hours.

Mixing Eclair Shells:

1. Bring 2 cups of water and shortening to a boil.
2. Add the bread flour to the boiling mixture and stir well until fully incorporated.
3. Remove the pan from the stove and cool the mixture for 10 minutes.
4. Add the eggs, one at a time, slowly until mixed in.
5. Dissolve the baking ammonia in ½ cup of water.
6. Mix the water mixture in the dough.

7. Place the dough mixture in a pastry bag fitted with a medium sized plain tube.
8. Pipe the dough in the shape of long fingers 2 inches apart on a parchment-lined baking sheet.
9. Place the baking sheet in the 400⁰ F preheated oven for about 10–15 minutes or until the shells are golden brown.
10. Move the baking sheet to a wire rack to cool.
11. Use a fingertip to make a hole on the end of each cooled shell.
12. Fill a pastry bag fitted with a medium sized plain tube with the custard and pipe it slowly into the hole.

Mixing Chocolate Glaze:
1. Using a wooden spoon, stir the water, corn syrup, and granulated sugar in a saucepan.
2. Bring the mixture to a full rolling boil over medium heat, stirring occasionally.
3. Remove from heat and add the chocolate pieces.
4. Let it sit about one minute until the chocolate is melted.
5. Whisk the glaze.
6. Dip the tops of the shells in the chocolate glaze.

Chocolate Nut Wafers

Yield: Approximately 2 ½ to 3 dozen cookies.

Ingredients:

4 ½ cups (19 oz.) confectioners' sugar
1 ½ cups (4.7 oz.) cocoa
1 ¼ cups (6 oz.) cake flour
1 ⅓ cups (9.6 oz.) shortening
4 eggs
1 tsp. vanilla extract
1 tsp. butter extract
¾ cup (3 oz.) pecans or walnuts,
 finely chopped

Directions:

1. Preheat oven to 375° F.
2. Have all ingredients at room temperature.
3. Grease and flour the baking sheet.
4. Whisk together the confectioners' sugar, cocoa, and cake flour in a mixing bowl.
5. Cream the whisked ingredients and shortening until a smooth paste.
6. Add the eggs, one at a time, while mixing.
7. Add the vanilla extract and butter extract and mix on low speed for 2 minutes.
8. Spread the mixture into the prepared baking sheet.
9. Place chopped nuts on top of the batter.
10. Place the baking sheet in the oven and bake the cookies for 8–10 minutes.
11. Cool for 5 minutes and then move the baking sheet to a wire rack to complete cooling.
12. Cut into 1-inch by 4-inch rectangles.

Almond Macaroon Cookies

Yield: Approximately 5 dozen cookies.

Ingredients:

25 oz. almond paste
1 ¾ cups (12.5 oz.) granulated sugar
3 cups (12.5 oz.) confectioners' sugar
10 egg whites

Directions:

1. Preheat oven to 340⁰ F.
2. Have all ingredients at room temperature.
3. Break the almond paste into small pieces.
4. Mix the almond paste, granulated sugar, and confectioners' sugar until smooth.
5. Add the egg whites slowly and mix on low speed for 2 minutes.
6. Using a pastry bag fitted with a star tube, pipe the batter the size of a quarter onto a parchment-lined baking sheet, 2 inches apart.
7. Place the baking sheet in the oven and bake for 11 minutes or until the cookie bottoms are lightly browned.
8. Move the baking sheet to a wire rack to let the cookies cool before removing them from the parchment paper.
9. If the cookies are stuck to the parchment paper, turn the parchment paper over and brush the back with water.

Hermit Cookies

Yield: Approximately 3 dozen cookies.

Ingredients:

¾ cup (5.6 oz.) light brown sugar
1 cup (7.5 oz.) shortening
1 egg
1 tsp. vanilla extract
½ tsp. butter extract
2 ½ cups (12 oz.) cake flour
½ tsp. salt
⅔ tsp. baking soda
½ cup hot water
½ cup (1.9 oz.) pecans, chopped
3 ¼ cups (16.9 oz.) dates, pitted
  and chopped

Directions:

1. Preheat oven to 350⁰ F.
2. Have all ingredients at room temperature.
3. In a mixing bowl, cream the brown sugar and shortening on low speed for 2 minutes.
4. Add the egg to the creamed mixture and mix until blended.
5. Mix in the vanilla extract and the butter extract.
6. In a separate bowl, whisk together the cake flour, salt, and baking soda.
7. Add the whisked ingredients to the batter and mix until combined.
8. Mix in ½ cup of hot water.
9. Fold in the chopped pecans and chopped dates.
10. Using a No. 30 (1 Tbs.) cookie scoop, scoop the cookies and place 2 inches apart on a parchment-lined baking sheet.
11. Place the baking sheet in the oven and bake the cookies for approximately 10 minutes or until the edges are firm.
12. Move the baking sheet to a wire rack to cool for 10 minutes. Slide the parchment onto a wire rack to finish cooling.

FALL SEASON

FALL SEASON

The fall season was my favorite. The bakery's sugar cookies (shaped like bats, cats, and pumpkins) and the cupcakes (topped with orange or chocolate icing and stick witches and pumpkins) were in demand for school Halloween parties. Rita and I had our own special pre-Halloween treat. Every October 30th, my father would bring home two birthday cakes, iced white and decorated with orange pumpkins and black cats and witches, to celebrate our birthday.

Once, Mama hosted a birthday party for Rita and me when we were very young. Afterwards, Mama said there would be no more birthday parties because she felt bad about guests having to bring two gifts. A couple of years later, my sister and I decided we wanted a party, and we invited several friends to come to our house after school on October 30th. Well, Mama was not pleased. She sent the children home, and my sister and I received a spanking for our birthday. Not exactly the birthday presents we had expected!

Trick-or-treating was a safe time for kids then, and all the neighborhood children participated. The Olde Presbyterian Church Cemetery at 307 West Gay Street was a favorite spot because we trick-or-treaters imagined spirits rising from graves, some dating back to the 1800s. On one Halloween, I remember arriving home with my bag of treats and finding my mother in the kitchen. She was busy with cutting and wrapping slices of birthday cakes for the last round of trick-or-treating ghosts and goblins. Without enough candy left to go around, Mama wanted to be sure every child received a treat.

Fall was also football season, and the citizens of Lancaster flocked to the Friday night home games. My father was busy working, so my parents could not take Rita and me to the games. But I had my own way of enjoying those Friday nights. I remember standing in front of the large picture window in our living room, watching fans walk to the Roach Stewart Field behind Lancaster High School on the corner of Wylie and York Streets, and hearing the loud, energetic band music playing during the halftime show.

Besides cheering on Lancaster's football team from our living room, I have another special memory involving my brother Donald and some of his friends, also high school athletes. Often Donald would invite them to our home after school. Whenever William "Punchy" McGuirt and Harold McManus visited, I was totally awestruck but too shy to say anything. Without a doubt, on those days I felt my first pangs of Puppy Love.

The Thanksgiving holiday brought sugar cookies shaped liked turkeys, pecan pies, sweet potato pies, and pumpkin pies.

RECIPES

Basic Figure Cookies

Yield: Approximately 2 dozen cookies.

Ingredients:

3 ⅓ cups (16.3 oz.) cake flour
1 tsp. (.17 oz.) baking powder
1 ¾ cups (12.2 oz.) granulated sugar
⅓ tsp. salt
1 cup (6.8 oz.) shortening
3 eggs
2 tsp. lemon extract
½ tsp. vanilla extract

Optional Ingredients for Chocolate Bats and Cats Cookies:
* *Add 1 ¼ tsp. baking soda to the cake flour and baking powder.*
* *Substitute 1 cup cocoa powder for the lemon and vanilla flavorings, and whisk the cocoa powder into the flour mixture.*

Directions:

1. Have all ingredients at room temperature.
2. Whisk together the cake flour and baking powder *(optional soda and cocoa for chocolate bats and cats)* and set aside.
3. Cream the granulated sugar, salt, and shortening on low speed until a smooth paste forms.
4. Add the eggs, one at a time, and blend on low speed.
5. Add the lemon extract and vanilla extract while blending on low speed.
6. Add the flour mixture and mix on low until just combined.
7. Divide the dough into two pieces.
8. Wrap each piece in plastic wrap and shape into a disk.

9. Refrigerate the dough at least 2 hours.
10. Place the dough one piece at a time on lightly floured surface and roll out to ⅛ inch thick.
11. Cut out the cookies, using figure cookie cutters.
12. Place the cookies 2 inches apart on a parchment-lined baking sheet.
13. Place the baking sheet in the refrigerator 20–30 minutes to prevent the cookies from spreading while baking.
14. Preheat oven to 375⁰ F.
15. Place the baking sheet in the oven and bake the cookies for 8–10 minutes.
16. Move the baking sheet to a wire rack to cool for 10 minutes.
17. Slide the parchment onto a wire rack to finish cooling.

Ice Box Cookies

Yield: Approximately 2 ½ to 3 dozen cookies.

Ingredients:

2 ⅓ cups (16.3 oz.) granulated sugar
⅔ tsp. salt
1 ½ tsp. (.25 oz.) baking soda
1 ⅓ cups (10.2 oz.) shortening
1 ½ tsp. ground cinnamon
1 tsp. vanilla extract
1 tsp. butter extract
3 eggs
2 ⅔ Tbs. (2 oz.) molasses
3 ⅓ cups (16.3 oz.) cake flour
¼ cup (1 ½ oz.) mixed nuts,
 finely chopped
⅓ cup (2 oz.) peanuts, finely chopped

Directions:

1. Cream the sugar, salt, soda, shortening, cinnamon, vanilla extract, and butter extract on low speed for 3 minutes.
2. Add the eggs, one at a time, and mix on low speed for 2 minutes.
3. Add the molasses and mix on low speed for 2 minutes.
4. Sift in the flour and mix 1 minute while scraping down sides and bottom of the bowl.
5. Add the chopped nuts and mix in, just until blended.
6. Shape the dough into long, square-shaped cylinders about 2 inches in diameter.
7. Wrap the dough in plastic wrap, place on baking sheet, and refrigerate for several hours or overnight.
8. Slice the dough ¼ inch thick and place on parchment-lined baking sheet 2 inches apart.
9. Place the baking sheet in a 375⁰ F preheated oven for 8–10 minutes.
10. Move the baking sheet to a wire rack to cool for 10 minutes.
11. Slide the parchment onto a wire rack to finish cooling.

Mealy Pie Dough

Yield: 4 9-inch pie crusts.

The mealy pie dough is best used for the bottom crust because it doesn't absorb liquid from pie fillings and becomes soggy like flaky pie dough.

Flaky pie dough can be used for the top crust. (Buck used mealy pie dough for both the top and bottom crusts.) For flaky pie dough, rub the shortening into the flour just until little lumps about the size of peas are formed.

Ingredients:

3 ¼ cups (15.5 oz.) cake flour
1 ¼ cups (8.6 oz.) shortening
2 tsp. salt
2 Tbs. nonfat milk powder
⅔ cup ice water

Egg wash:

1 egg beaten with 1 Tbs. water
    or milk

Directions:

1. Sift the flour into a mixing bowl.
2. Add the shortening and rub in the flour until the mixture is the consistency of cornmeal.
3. Dissolve the salt and milk powder in the ice water.
4. Add the water to the dough mixture and mix very slightly.
5. Wrap the dough in plastic wrap and refrigerate for 3–4 hours.
6. Dust the counter and rolling pin with a small amount of flour.
7. Flatten the dough slightly and roll out in a circle to just under ¼ inch thick. Place a 9-inch pie plate upside down on the dough circle. The circle should be about 2 inches larger than the pie plate.
8. Fold the dough into fourths and unfold the dough in the pie plate. Press the dough into the corners without stretching.

Single crust pie with a fluted edge:

Leave about ¼ inch excess dough around the rim. Pinch the dough into a ridge, using the thumb and forefinger of both hands. Pinch at 1-inch intervals to make the crust fluted. Prick the bottom of the crust with a fork for steam to escape.

Baked pie crust:

Preheat oven to 475⁰ F and bake the pie crust for 8–10 minutes.

Two Crust Pie:

1. Roll out the dough for the top crust as above.
2. Drop the dough on top of the pie filling.
3. Brush the rim of the bottom crust with egg wash.
4. Seal both edges firmly and remove excess dough.
5. Flute or crimp rims.
6. Cut three slits in the top crust for the steam to escape.
7. Brush the top crust with egg wash.

Pecan Pie Filling

Yield: 1 9–inch pie.

Ingredients:

2 cups (15.6 oz.) packed brown sugar
½ tsp. salt
¼ cup (1.2 oz.) cornstarch
¼ cup (1 oz.) cake flour
2 eggs
⅔ cup hot water
¼ cup (1.7 oz.) shortening melted
⅓ tsp. vanilla extract
½ cup (1 ⅔ oz.) pecan halves

Directions:

1. Mix the brown sugar, salt, cornstarch, and flour in a mixing bowl.
2. Add the eggs, one at a time, on low speed until blended.
3. Add the hot water to the mixture and blend in.
4. Mix in the melted shortening and the vanilla extract.
5. Pour the cooled filling into an unbaked 9-inch Mealy Pie Dough bottom crust *(see page 36)*.
6. Cover the top of the filling with the pecan halves.
7. Place the pan in a 425⁰ F preheated oven for 10 minutes.
8. Lower the oven temperature to 325⁰ F.
9. Continue baking about 35 minutes until the custard is set.

Sweet Potato Pie Filling

Yield: 1 9-inch pie.

Ingredients:

2 ½ cups sweet potatoes, cooked
  and mashed or canned sweet
  potatoes mashed
1 ¼ cups (8.5 oz.) granulated sugar
½ tsp. salt
⅛ tsp. ground cinnamon
2 ½ Tbs. (.71 oz.) cornstarch
1 ½ Tbs. (.71 oz.) shortening, melted
¾ Tbs. (.35 oz.) margarine
3 eggs
⅔ cup water
½ tsp. vanilla extract
½ tsp. butter extract

Directions:

1. Preheat oven to 450⁰ F.
2. Mix cooled potatoes, sugar, salt, cinnamon, and cornstarch on medium speed until smooth.
3. Add the melted shortening and margarine and mix until blended in.
4. Add the eggs and mix in.
5. Mix in the water, vanilla extract, and butter extract.
6. Let the mixture sit for about 30 minutes and then stir.
7. Add the mixture to a 9-inch unbaked Mealy Pie Dough bottom crust *(see page 36)*.
8. Bake at 450⁰ F for 15 minutes. Then lower the temperature to 350⁰ F and bake approximately 30–40 minutes or until a knife inserted in the middle comes out clean.

Lemon Pie Filling

Yield: 1 9-inch pie.

Ingredients:

For Lemon Filling:
1 ⅔ cups (12 oz.) granulated sugar
½ tsp. (.09 oz.) citric acid
2 ¼ Tbs. (1.1 oz.) margarine
2 ½ cups (21 oz.) cold water
⅓ cup (3 oz.) warm water
2 eggs
½ cup (2.4 oz.) ClearJel (may substitute cornstarch)
5 Tbs. (1 ½ oz.) lemon juice powder

For Meringue:
8 egg whites
12 oz. granulated sugar

Directions:
1. Prepare a 9-inch baked Mealy Pie Dough bottom crust *(see page 36)*.
2. Pour the cooled lemon filling into the cooled pie crust.
3. Spread the meringue over the filled pie crust.
4. Bake in 375⁰ F oven until the meringue is set and nicely browned.

Mixing Lemon Filling:
1. Bring to a boil the granulated sugar, citric acid, margarine, and cold water.
2. In a separate bowl, mix the warm water, eggs, ClearJel, and lemon powder until the ClearJel and lemon powder are dissolved.
3. Add the egg mixture to the boiling mixture and cook until thickened.

Mixing Meringue:
1. With a whip attachment, beat the egg whites on medium speed and then high speed until soft peaks form.
2. Add the granulated sugar slowly and whip until stiff.

Egg Custard Pie Filling

Yield: 1 9-inch pie.

Ingredients:

1 ⅔ Tbs. (.5 oz.) cake flour
½ cup (4 oz.) granulated sugar
1 ¾ Tbs. (.5 oz.) cornstarch
¼ cup (1.3 oz.) nonfat milk powder
1 ½ Tbs. (.67 oz.) shortening melted
1 tsp. vanilla extract
Pinch of salt
2 eggs
1 ¼ cups hot water

Directions:

1. Preheat oven to 325⁰ F.
2. Mix the cake flour, granulated sugar, cornstarch, milk powder, shortening, vanilla extract, and salt in a bowl.
3. Add the eggs, one at a time, until blended.
4. Add the hot water and mix until smooth.
5. Pour the filling into an unbaked Mealy Pie Dough bottom crust *(see page 36)*.
6. Place the pan in the oven and bake for 45–55 minutes until a knife inserted in the center comes out clean.

WINTER SEASON

Rev. J.W. McElrath, second from left; E.N. Courtney, third from left

WINTER SEASON

Christmas

The weeks before Christmas were the busiest and most profitable time of the year for local merchants, especially when the textile mill gave bonuses to the employees. My father worked twenty-one hours a day, just to keep up with the demand for sweets and breads. He doubled and sometimes tripled the output of the regular batches of baked goods. Fragrant smells emanated from two huge gas-powered wall ovens into the surrounding neighborhoods.

Imagine the hard work required for all of the holiday baking! Two to three hundred dozen brown and serve biscuits, tea biscuits, Parker House rolls, and loaves of bread had to be manually wrapped for sale. The thousands of cakes, pies, cookies, brownies, donuts, pastries, and cupcakes that were cooked ahead had to be retrieved from subzero freezers whenever retail display cases emptied. Often the crowds of customers in the retail area made it difficult for employees to transport goods from the production area to the display cases. At the same time, the phone would ring constantly with hundreds of orders to be filled. This was an exhausting but rewarding time of the year for our family and all employees.

My grandfather was a kind soul. Every Christmas he donated carloads of cakes and pies to local charities. The Rev. J.W. McElrath, pastor of Grace Methodist Church, distributed the baked goods to needy families.

On Christmas morning, Santa typically left each of us children a special envelope with money or a present under the tree. After opening presents, the family would enjoy a delicious Christmas lunch of homemade cornbread dressing, ham, green beans, and other trimmings. In the week following Christmas, the bakery was closed for all employees to rest and to welcome the New Year with their families.

The Christmas of 1959 was especially memorable for both good and bad reasons. Santa brought Rita and me our first bicycles. Unlike any of our friends' bicycles, ours were much taller with brakes on the handlebars. Daddy said they were English bicycles and told us to ride only on the sidewalks, not in the streets. After several days of trying to master the bikes in the yard, Rita and I bravely headed toward the sidewalk to circle the block. As I approached Mrs. Jones's house on York Street, I saw her gathered with several people on her walkway. A split second later, the elderly Mrs. Jones stepped onto the sidewalk and was run over by me and my English bicycle! People rushed to get the bike and me off Mrs. Jones. While Mrs. Jones was able to stand and walk, I could do neither. Rita didn't stop and continued circling the block. Someone called my mother, and she loaded the bike and me into our big-finned Dodge for the ride to Dr. Horton's office. My tibia was broken. Now with a heavy plaster cast from my toes to my hip, I spent eight weeks in a wheelchair and two weeks on crutches. Still, I have to thank the neighborhood boys who took turns pushing me to and from elementary school in January and into February. By the way, the bike fared better than I did, and it proved useful to me for several more years.

I was glad to see the end of 1959, which also brought an end to my music lessons. Only two months before Christmas, I had a cast removed from my dominant left arm, broken when I had slipped on a doormat while leaving school. Then came my bike accident. I had initially been frustrated over not being able to play bass because of my arm cast, and then later I was even more frustrated about not being able to reach to the keyboard easily with my hip cast. So, I quit piano lessons with Mrs. Buddy Montgomery. Somehow, I knew 1960 would be a better year for me!

Valentine's Day

Valentine's Day was always a special treat every year in elementary school. Prior to Valentine's Day, we students decorated shoe boxes to hold Valentine cards from our classmates and made a list of classmates' names for addressing our Valentine cards. Our teachers encouraged us to send cards to all classmates. Nevertheless, the popular students typically received more cards than some of our other classmates. It was heartbreaking for those in the latter group. After we had distributed the cards, we all consumed Valentine sweets provided by our mothers, who had volunteered to provide refreshments for special class occasions.

After school, I felt special because I received fancy cards and small, heart-shaped boxes of candy from my neighborhood sweethearts. Making me feel even more special was my father giving boxes of chocolates to my mother, Rita, and me. In fact, my dear father continued to give me a box of chocolates on Valentine's Day until his death in 1990.

George Washington's Birthday

In 1962, local merchants held a George Washington's Birthday promotion, which included drawings to win two-tier George Washington birthday cakes that the bakery would provide to the local merchants. Since no rules excluded bakery family members or employees of the bakery from registering for the prized cakes, I made the rounds with my friends to local businesses and registered to win a cake. Well, that was the first and only contest I have ever won! Not everyone was pleased. For several days afterward, the phone rang constantly at our house because the majority of Lancaster citizens thought I should return the cake. However, after considering all of the arguments, pro and con, my parents decided to let me keep the cake. On the following Saturday night, I invited several classmates to our house to listen to Frankie Valli and the Four Seasons, do the Limbo, and eat cake.

RECIPES

Christmas Tree Figure Cookies

*U*se the recipe for Basic Figure Cookies *(see page 33)*. Add green food coloring to the dough. I recommend using gel food coloring because it is more concentrated than liquid food coloring, therefore minimizing the amount of liquid added to recipes. Cut out the dough using a tree-shaped cookie cutter. Wash the tops of the cookies with an egg wash. Decorate with red and green Christmas sprinkles prior to baking or dip the tops of the cooled cookies in a glaze of 1 Tbs. milk and ½ cup of confectioners' sugar.

Red Heart Figure Cookies

Use the recipe for Basic Figure Cookies *(see page 33)*. Add red food coloring to the dough. Cut out the dough using a heart-shaped cookie cutter. Wash the tops of the cookies with an egg wash and decorate with red sprinkles prior to baking or dip the tops of the cooled cookies in a glaze of 1 Tbs. milk and ½ cup of confectioners' sugar.

Cherry Pies

Use the recipe for the Mealy Pie Dough two-crust pie *(see page 36)*. Spoon 2 cans of cherry pie filling on the bottom crust. One tsp. of almond extract or cinnamon extract can be stirred in the cherry pie filling to enhance the flavor. Place the top pie crust over the cherry filling and seal the edge. Brush the top crust with egg wash or melted butter prior to baking and cut several slits in the top crust. Another option to make the pie special is to use a small cookie cutter to cut shapes out of the top crust. Bake in 425° F preheated oven until the top is lightly browned and the cherry filling is bubbling through the top slits or shapes, about 30–40 minutes.

Yellow Layer Cake

Yield: 3 8-inch cake layers; 2 9-inch cake layers; or 3 dozen cupcakes.

Ingredients:

3 ½ cups (16.6 oz.) cake flour
2 ⅛ Tbs. (1.04 oz.) baking powder
⅓ cup (1.7 oz.) nonfat milk powder
2 tsp. (.41 oz.) salt
1 cup (7.5 oz.) shortening
3 cups (20.7 oz.) granulated sugar
6 eggs
2 tsp. vanilla extract
¼ tsp. lemon extract
¼ tsp. butter extract
1 ⅓ cups (11 oz.) water (divided into ¾ cup and ⅔ cup)

Optional Conversion to Devil's Food Cake:

1. *Sift ½ cup cocoa powder, 1 ¾ Tbs. sugar, and 1 ¼ tsp. baking soda into the dry ingredients.*

Directions:

1. Grease pans and dust with flour.
2. Have all ingredients at room temperature.
3. Sift the cake flour, baking powder, milk powder, and salt into a mixing bowl.
4. Add the shortening and mix on low speed for 2 minutes.
5. Stop the mixer and scrape down the sides of the mixing bowl and continue mixing for 2 minutes.
6. Sift the sugar into the mixing bowl, add ¾ cup of water, and mix on low speed for 3-5 minutes. Scrape down the sides of the mixing bowl several times.
7. In a separate bowl, lightly beat the eggs, and blend in ⅔ cup of water, vanilla extract, lemon extract, and butter extract.
8. Add this mixture to the cake batter in 3 parts. Stop the mixer after adding each part to scrape down the sides of the mixing bowl.
9. Continue mixing on low speed for 5 minutes.
10. If you are using 8-inch round pans or 9-inch round pans, bake in 350⁰ F preheated oven for 25–30 minutes.
11. If you are making cupcakes, fill the lined muffin pans ⅔ full and bake at 350⁰ F for 18–20 minutes.
12. The cake is done when a toothpick inserted in the center comes out clean.
13. Cool the cake in the pans for 15 minutes prior to turning cake onto wire racks to cool.

White Layer Cake

Yield: 3 8-inch cake layers; 2 9-inch cake layers; or 3 ½ dozen cupcakes.

Ingredients:

3 ⅛ cups (15.3 oz.) cake flour
2 Tbs. (.96 oz.) baking powder
⅓ cup (1.5 oz.) nonfat milk powder
2 ¼ tsp. (.48 oz.) salt
1 cup (7.6 oz.) shortening
2 ⅔ cups (18.4 oz.) granulated sugar
11 egg whites
2 ½ tsp. (.38 oz.) vanilla extract
¼ tsp. lemon extract (may substitute almond extract)
1 ⅓ cups (11 oz.) water (divided into ¾ cup and ⅔ cup)

Directions:

1. Grease pans and dust with flour.
2. Have all ingredients at room temperature.
3. Sift the cake flour, baking powder, milk powder, and salt into a mixing bowl.
4. Add the shortening and mix on low speed for 2 minutes.
5. Stop the mixer and scrape down the sides of the mixing bowl and continue mixing for 2 minutes.
6. Sift the sugar into the mixing bowl, add ¾ cup of water, and mix on low speed for 3-5 minutes. Scrape down the sides of the mixing bowl several times.
7. In a separate bowl, lightly beat the egg whites, and blend in ⅔ cup of water, vanilla extract, and lemon extract.
8. Add this mixture to the cake batter in 3 parts. Stop the mixer after adding each part to scrape down the sides of the mixing bowl.
9. Continue mixing on low speed for 5 minutes.
10. If you are using 8-inch round pans or 9-inch round pans, bake in 350⁰ F preheated oven for 25–30 minutes.
11. If you are making cupcakes, fill the lined muffin pans ⅔ full and bake at 350⁰ F for 18–20 minutes.
12. The cake is done when a toothpick inserted in the center comes out clean.
13. Cool the cake in the pans for 15 minutes prior to turning cake onto wire racks to cool.

Chocolate Icing

Ingredients:

1 ⅓ cups (4 oz.) cocoa
½ cup (4 oz.) shortening,
   divided in half
4 ¾ cups (20 oz.) sifted
   confectioners' sugar
2 ⅔ Tbs. (2 oz.) light corn syrup
Pinch of salt
⅓ cup warm water
1 tsp. vanilla extract

Directions:

1. Place the cocoa and ¼ cup of shortening in a mixing bowl.
2. Place ¼ cup of shortening in a saucepan and heat to 130⁰ F.
3. Add the melted shortening to the cocoa mixture and mix until smooth.
4. In a separate bowl, whisk together the confectioners' sugar, corn syrup, salt, warm water, and vanilla.
5. Add the sugar mixture to the cocoa mixture and mix until smooth.

Chocolate Fudge Icing

Ingredients:

5 oz. unsweetened chocolate
½ cup (4 oz.) shortening
¼ cup (1 oz.) cake flour
1 tsp. salt
11 ¾ cups (50 oz.) confectioners' sugar
   (divided, 1 ¼ cups (5 oz.) and 10 ⅔
   cups (45 oz.))
1 ⅓ Tbs. (1 oz.) honey
1 tsp. vanilla extract
½ tsp. chocolate flavoring
Hot water, variable

Directions:

1. Melt the chocolate and shortening over boiling water in a double boiler (no hotter than 110⁰ F) and let cool to room temperature.
2. Whisk together the cake flour, salt, and 1 ¼ cups confectioners' sugar in a mixing bowl and set aside.
3. In a separate bowl, mix together 10 ⅔ cups confectioners' sugar, honey, vanilla extract, chocolate flavoring, and ¾ cup hot water. Add this mixture to the whisked ingredients and mix until smooth.
4. Add ¼ cup of hot water as needed for a smooth consistency.
5. Barely mix in the melted chocolate and shortening.

Japanese Fruit Cake

Yield: 1 8-inch cake

Ingredients:

For Cake:
1 ¾ cups (10.7 oz.) raisins
2 ⅔ cups (8 oz.) dried apples
2 cups (16 oz.) water
2 cups (13.3 oz.) granulated sugar
⅔ cup (4.7 oz.) shortening
½ cup (2 oz.) nonfat milk powder
3 eggs
3 cups (14.7 oz.) cake flour
¾ cup (5.3 oz.) spice mix

For Spice Mix:
¾ cup (3.6 oz.) cake flour
1 ⅓ Tbs. (.63 oz.) baking soda
1 ½ Tbs. (.75 oz.) baking powder
¾ Tbs. (.16 oz.) mace
¾ Tbs. (.16 oz.) allspice
1 ⅓ Tbs. (.36 oz.) cinnamon
1 ⅔ tsp. (.36 oz.) salt

Add all the ingredients together and sift six times.

For Icing:
2 Tbs. (.5 oz.) cornstarch
12 oz. water (divided, ½ cup and 1 cup)
2 cups (14.1 oz.) granulated sugar
1 Tbs. vanilla extract
1 Tbs. lemon juice
1 pkg. frozen shredded coconut, thawed

Directions:

1. Soak the raisins and apples in 2 cups of water overnight.
2. Grease and flour 3 8-inch round pans.
3. Have all ingredients at room temperature.
4. Cream the granulated sugar, shortening, and milk powder until light while keeping the sides of bowl scraped down.
5. Gradually add the eggs and mix until light and fluffy.
6. Add ½ of the soak and mix until blended in.
7. Add the cake flour and spice mix and mix until blended in.
8. Add the remaining soak of apples and raisins and mix until smooth.
9. Pour the batter into prepared cake pans.
10. Smooth the batter with a spatula to evenly distribute batter in pans.
11. Tap the pans on the counter to remove air bubbles.
12. Bake in 375⁰ F preheated oven 25 minutes or until a toothpick inserted in the center comes out clean.
13. Cool at least 15 minutes before turning the layers onto wire racks for additional cooling time.

14. Brush excess crumbs from the cooled cake layers. Place the bottom layer flat side up on a cake board or platter.
15. Stir the icing and spread it on top of the layer to the edges.
16. Place the middle layer over the bottom layer, flat side up, and spread icing on the top of the layer to the edges.
17. Place the top layer over the middle layer, rounded side up.
18. Using a spatula, place the icing on the center of the top layer and spread to the edges and down the sides of the cake.
19. Press the shredded coconut on the top and sides of the cake.

Mixing Icing:
1. Dissolve the cornstarch in ½ cup of the water and set aside.
2. Bring 1 cup water to a boil in a saucepan on the stove.
3. Stir in the granulated sugar, vanilla extract, and lemon juice.
4. Boil mixture to 236^0 F, stirring often.
5. Stir in the dissolved cornstarch.
6. Cook over medium-high heat, stirring constantly until the mixture is thickened.
7. Remove the icing from the heat.
8. Let it cool prior to icing the cake.

German Chocolate Cake

Yield: 1 9-inch cake or 1 8-inch cake.

Ingredients:

For Cake:
3 ⅓ cups (16.4 oz.) cake flour
1 ¾ Tbs. (.85 oz.) baking powder
1 tsp. (.17 oz.) baking soda
½ cup (1.7 oz.) cocoa powder
1 ⅔ tsp. (.34 oz.) salt
2 ⅔ cups (19.1 oz.) granulated sugar
  (divided into 2 ⅓ cups and ⅓ cup)
¾ cup (5.5 oz.) shortening
⅓ cup (2.7 oz.) margarine
2 eggs
⅔ cup water
1 ⅓ cups (11 oz.) buttermilk
4 egg whites

For Icing:
1 ¾ cups evaporated milk
2 ¼ cups brown sugar, packed
½ cup margarine
3 eggs
⅔ cup sweetened shredded coconut
1 cup (3 ½ oz.) chopped pecans

Directions:

1. Preheat oven to 350⁰ F.
2. Have all ingredients at room temperature.
3. Grease 2 9-inch pans or 3 8-inch pans.
4. Line the bottoms of the pans with parchment paper, and grease the parchment paper.
5. Whisk the cake flour, baking powder, baking soda, cocoa powder, and salt into a medium bowl and set aside.
6. In another bowl, cream the 2 ⅓ cups of granulated sugar, shortening, and margarine until light and fluffy.
7. Add the eggs, one at a time, to the sugar mixture and mix until blended.
8. In another bowl, mix the water and buttermilk.
9. Beat ½ of the flour mixture into the cake batter, just until smooth on low speed. Beat in ½ of the buttermilk until smooth.
10. Add the remaining flour and mix just until smooth. Beat in the remaining buttermilk just until smooth.

11. Using a clean bowl and mixing beaters, beat egg whites and ⅓ cup of granulated sugar on high speed until stiff peaks form.
12. Using a spatula, fold the egg white mixture into the cake batter until blended.
13. Pour the batter into the prepared cake pans.
14. Smooth the batter with a spatula to evenly distribute the batter in the pans.
15. Tap the pans on the counter to remove air bubbles.
16. Place the pans in the preheated oven, and bake 30–35 minutes for the 9-inch pans or bake 35–40 minutes for the 8-inch pans. The cake is done when a toothpick inserted into the center comes out clean.
17. Cool the cake in the pans for about 10–15 minutes.
18. Invert the pans onto the cooling rack, and then invert right side up onto another cooling rack. Cool completely before icing.
19. Brush excess crumbs from the cooled cake layers. Place the bottom layer, flat side up, on a cake board or platter.
20. Spread the cooled icing on the top of the layer to the edges.
21. Place the middle layer over the bottom layer, flat side up, and spread icing on the top of the layer to the edges.
22. Place the top layer over the middle layer, rounded side up.
23. Using a spatula, place the icing on the center of the top layer and spread to the edges and down the sides of the cake.

Mixing Icing:
1. Cook evaporated milk, brown sugar, and margarine in a saucepan over moderately low heat, whisking frequently until smooth.
2. Add the eggs and cook over moderately low heat, whisking frequently until thickened.
3. Stir in the sweetened shredded coconut and pecans.

Ginger Boys

Yield: Approximately 2 ½ dozen 4–inch cookies.

Ingredients:

2 cups (13.5 oz.) granulated sugar
¾ cup (6.7 oz.) light brown sugar, packed *(may use dark brown sugar for a little darker, caramelized cookie)*
½ tsp. (.11 oz.) salt
2 tsp. (.31 oz.) baking soda
1 ¾ tsp. (.11 oz.) ground ginger
1 cup (6.7 oz.) shortening
2 ¼ tsp. (.21 oz.) ground cinnamon
⅔ tsp. vanilla extract
⅔ tsp. butter extract
4 eggs
1 ¾ Tbs. (1.3 oz.) molasses
4 ¼ cups (20.2 oz.) cake flour

Directions:

1. Have all ingredients at room temperature.
2. Cream the granulated sugar, brown sugar, salt, soda, ginger, shortening, cinnamon, vanilla extract, and butter extract at low speed until the mixture is a smooth paste.
3. Add the eggs, one at a time, while mixing.
4. Add the molasses and mix on low speed until blended.
5. Add the flour and mix until just blended in the mixture.
6. Divide the dough into two pieces.
7. Wrap each piece in plastic wrap and shape into a disk.
8. Refrigerate the dough overnight.
9. Preheat the oven to 360⁰ F.
10. Place the dough one piece at a time on lightly floured surface, and roll out the dough just under ¼ inch thick.
11. Using a gingerbread boy cookie cutter, cut out ginger boys, and place on a parchment-lined baking sheet 2 inches apart.
12. Place the baking sheet in the oven, and bake for 8-10 minutes or until the edges and bottoms of the cookies are brown.
13. Move the baking sheet to a wire rack to cool for 10 minutes. Slide parchment onto a wire rack to finish cooling.
14. Decorate as desired.

SPRING SEASON

SPRING SEASON

*E*aster was the second busiest holiday for the bakery. Lancaster awoke from its winter sleep, showing off its spring finery, and everyone planned for a special Easter meal. The bakery helped with the celebrations at the elementary schools and churches by providing rabbit-shaped sugar cookies; cupcakes decorated with green icing, coconut, and jellybeans; and small egg-shaped dipped cakes, decorated with colorful flower buds made out of icing. At our house, in addition to baskets filled with candy, the Easter bunny left lovely corsages on the front porch for my mother, Rita, and me to wear with our Easter finery to church. During the Easter service at the First United Methodist Church, the Youth Choir joined the Adult Choir to sing hymns and anthems.

One Easter when I was in elementary school, I begged my mother to let me have an Easter egg party in our backyard on Good Friday. I was so happy when she said yes, and I set out to plan the best-ever Easter egg party. I delivered my own handmade invitations to my fifth-grade elementary school friends. I boiled eggs, dipped them in colorful dyes, and hid them in the yard for my guests to find. The one lucky guest who found the "golden" egg would win a bunny cake from the bakery. Carefully I set up card tables to hold our drinks and Easter cookies and cupcakes. Unfortunately, my big mistake was not including Rita in my planning. She terrorized my party, spit in the drinks, pushed guests, and pulled their hair. I think now that I was too young to be aware of how much Rita often felt excluded. Of course, my guests went home. Heartbroken and embarrassed, I vowed never to host another party and never did as a child. Later as a mother, I happily hosted many birthday parties for my sons.

During the week of Mother's Day, the bakery's bestseller was a twelve-inch coconut cake decorated with one long-stem red rose.

RECIPES

Rabbit Figure Cookies

Use the recipe for Basic Figure Cookies *(see page 33)* and cut out the cookies using a rabbit-shaped cookie cutter. Then wash the dough with an egg wash, sprinkle with colored sugar, and make eyes by sticking a dark raisin in the face prior to baking.

Easter Cupcakes

Bake cupcakes using either the Yellow Layer Cake recipe *(see page 51)* or the White Layer Cake recipe *(see page 52)*. Add green food coloring to the buttercream icing *(see page 15)* prior to icing the cupcakes. Add a few drops of green food coloring to sweetened shredded coconut and sprinkle on top of the iced cupcakes. Top each cupcake with a few colorful jellybeans. Cut "handles" that measure 6 inches by ¼ inch from green construction paper, and press each end into the top of the cupcake to mimic the look of an Easter basket.

Coconut Macaroon Cookies

Yield: Approximately 3 dozen cookies.

Ingredients:

¾ cup water
½ cup (6 oz.) light corn syrup
2 ½ cups (18 oz.) granulated sugar
⅛ tsp. salt
5 ½ cups (18 oz.) macaroon coconut
6 egg whites
1 ⅛ tsp. (.19 oz.) baking powder
⅔ tsp. vanilla extract
⅔ tsp. butter extract
Candied cherries for garnish

Directions:

1. Preheat oven to 350⁰ F.
2. Line the baking sheet with parchment paper.
3. Add the water, corn syrup, sugar, and salt into a saucepan.
4. Bring to a boil on low heat to 120⁰ F, stirring constantly, and then remove the pan from the heat.
5. Add the coconut and blend.
6. Add slightly beaten egg whites and blend.
7. When the mixture is cool, blend in the baking powder, vanilla extract, and butter extract.
8. Using a pastry bag fitted with a star tube, pipe the batter about 1 inch in diameter onto the baking sheet, 2 inches apart.
9. Press ½ of a candied cherry in the center of each cookie.
10. Place the baking sheet in the preheated oven and bake for 15–20 minutes.
11. Slide the parchment paper onto a wire rack to cool.

Oatmeal Rocks Cookies

Yield: Approximately 5 dozen cookies.

Ingredients:

2 ⅓ cups (16.4 oz.) granulated sugar
1 ¼ tsp. salt
2 ⅛ tsp. (.34 oz.) baking soda
1 ½ cups (10.9 oz.) shortening
2 ⅓ Tbs. (.67 oz.) nonfat milk powder
⅔ cup (2.3 oz.) vanilla pound cake or
  vanilla Bundt cake, crumbled
1 tsp. vanilla extract
½ tsp. ground cinnamon
3 eggs
⅔ cups water
2 ⅓ cups (13.6 oz.) raisins
3 cups (5.5 oz.) rolled oats
⅓ cup (1 ½ oz.) pecans, chopped
3 ⅔ cups (17.7 oz.) bread flour

Directions:

1. Preheat oven to 400⁰ F.
2. Have all ingredients at room temperature.
3. Cream the granulated sugar, salt, baking soda, shortening, milk powder, cake crumbs, vanilla extract, and cinnamon on low speed for 3 minutes.
4. Add the eggs, one at a time, and mix on low speed for 2 minutes.
5. Add the water and mix on low speed until smooth.
6. Add the raisins, oats, and pecans, and mix on low speed until blended.
7. Sift in the bread flour and mix 1 minute or until smooth. Scrape down sides of the bowl while mixing.
8. Drop the dough using a No. 40 (1.75 Tbs.) cookie scoop onto the parchment-lined sheet pan.
9. Place the baking sheet into the preheated oven for 8–10 minutes or until bottom edges of the cookies are golden brown.
10. Move the baking sheet to a wire rack to cool for 15 minutes. Slide the parchment paper onto a wire rack to finish cooling.

Batch Brown & Serve Biscuits

Yield: Approximately 4 ½ dozen biscuits.

Ingredients:

For Sponge:
1 ⅔ tsp. (.24 oz.) active dry yeast
2 Tbs. warm water (110⁰ F) for yeast
½ Tbs. (.23 oz.) granulated sugar
1 cup warm water (110⁰ F)
1 ⅔ cups (7.8 oz.) bread flour
⅔ cup (4.8 oz.) shortening
⅔ cup (4.8 oz.) lard

For Dough:
1 ⅛ cups ice water
3 Tbs. (1.5 oz.) baking powder
⅓ cup (1.5 oz.) nonfat milk powder
½ Tbs. (.23 oz.) granulated sugar
2 tsp. salt
2 ¾ cups (13.5 oz.) cake flour

Directions:

Mixing Sponge:

1. Dissolve the yeast in 2 Tbs. warm water (110⁰ F) and set aside.
2. Add the sugar and 1 cup warm water to a mixing bowl and mix until the sugar is dissolved.
3. Add sifted bread flour. When partially mixed, add the dissolved yeast.
4. Add the shortening and lard and mix until smooth.
5. Cover the bowl with a towel and set aside for an hour.

Mixing Dough:

1. Add the ice water, baking powder, milk powder, granulated sugar, and salt to the sponge mixture. Mix for 2 minutes.
2. Add sifted cake flour and mix until the dough is smooth. (Dough should have a medium-soft consistency and release easily from the mixer bowl.)
3. Place the dough on a floured board and roll out ½ inch thick.
4. Cut out biscuits, using a 2-inch biscuit cutter. (Press the cutter straight down and do not twist.)
5. Place biscuits ½ inch apart on parchment-lined baking sheet or greased baking sheet.
6. Bake in 425⁰ F preheated oven until lightly brown, about 20 minutes.

Optional: Bake in 425⁰ F oven for 10 minutes. Cool and freeze. When ready to eat, thaw biscuits and bake in 425⁰ F preheated oven until lightly brown, about 10 minutes.

Coconut Cake

Yield: 1 9-inch cake or 1 8-inch cake.

Ingredients:

For Cake:
See the recipe for White Layer Cake
  (see page 52).

For Boiled Icing:
1 cup (8 oz.) water
3 ½ cups granulated sugar
⅛ tsp. salt
1 tsp. cream of tartar
⅓ cup (4 oz.) light corn syrup
8 egg whites
¾ tsp. vanilla extract
2 cups sweetened shredded coconut

For Simple Syrup:
(Buck spread simple syrup over split
  cake layers for a moister product.)
2 cups granulated sugar
3 cups water
2 Tbs. milk

Directions:

1. Follow the White Layer Cake
   recipe *(see page 52)* and bake
   2 9-inch cake layers or 3 8-inch
   cake layers.
2. Brush excess crumbs from cooled
   cake layers. Place the bottom
   layer, flat side up, on a cake board
   or platter.
3. Cut through the layer horizontally
   and remove the top half.
4. Spread up to ½ cup of the simple
   syrup over the layer.
5. Replace the top half layer.
6. Spread warm icing on top of one
   layer to the edges and sprinkle
   sweetened shredded coconut on
   top of the layer.
7. Repeat the above steps for slicing/
   icing the middle layer if you are
   baking a 3-layer cake.
8. Place the top layer over the bottom
   layer, rounded side up.
9. Cut through the layer horizontally
   and remove the top half.

10. Spread up to ½ cup of the simple syrup over the layer.
11. Replace the top half layer.
12. Using a spatula, place the icing on the center of the top layer and spread the icing to the edges and down the sides of the cake.
13. Apply shredded coconut generously onto the top and sides of the soft icing.

Mixing Icing:
1. Boil the water, granulated sugar, salt, cream of tartar, and corn syrup in a saucepan until a candy thermometer inserted into mixture registers 240^0 F.
2. While the syrup is boiling, beat the egg whites and vanilla until soft peaks are formed.
3. Pour the hot syrup into the beaten egg whites in a slow stream while constantly whipping until the icing is smooth.

Mixing Simple Syrup:
1. Bring the granulated sugar, water, and milk to a boil in a saucepan and simmer for 3 minutes until sugar is dissolved.
2. Remove the saucepan from the heat.

For Mother's Day, place a fresh, red rose bud or red carnation on the top center of the cake. Another option is to add a red rosebud made from icing on the top center of the cake with a green icing stem.

Brownies

Yield: Approximately 4 dozen brownies.

Ingredients:

3.3 oz. unsweetened chocolate, cut into small pieces

1 ¼ cup (7.7 oz.) shortening

2 ¾ cups chocolate pound cake or chocolate Bundt cake, crumbled

1 ¼ cups (9 oz.) brown sugar, packed

1 ¼ cups (9 oz.) granulated sugar

1 ¼ tsp. salt

½ cup (5 oz.) light corn syrup

4 eggs (3.5 oz.)

⅔ tsp. vanilla extract

2 Tbs. water

1 ½ cups (7.2 oz.) bread flour

1 ½ cups (7.2 oz.) cake flour

Optional: ½ cup (2 oz.) chopped pecans or walnuts.

Directions:

1. Preheat oven to 325⁰ F.
2. Melt the chocolate and shortening over boiling water in a double boiler (no hotter than 110⁰ F) and let cool to room temperature.
3. Mix the cake crumbs, brown sugar, granulated sugar, salt, and corn syrup until blended.
4. Mix in the eggs, vanilla, and water until blended.
5. Mix in cooled chocolate and shortening until blended.
6. Sift the bread flour and cake flour and fold in the mixture. *Optional: Fold in ½ cup of chopped nuts (pecans, walnuts, etc.).*
7. Grease and flour a half-sized sheet pan (9 x 13 inches).
8. Pour the batter into the pan and spread the batter evenly to the edges of the sheet pan.
9. Place the baking sheet in the preheated oven for 45–60 minutes or until a toothpick inserted in the middle comes out clean.
10. Cool in the pan and ice the brownies with a thin layer of Chocolate Fudge Icing *(see page 53).*
11. Cut the brownies into 2-inch squares.

Donuts

Yield: Approximately 2 dozen donuts.

Ingredients:

For Donuts:
¼ cup water for yeast
1 ⅛ Tbs. (.48 oz.) active dry yeast
1 cup (4.9 oz.) cake flour
2 ⅓ cups (11.5 oz.) bread flour
1 ⅔ tsp. salt
⅔ Tbs. (.34 oz.) baking powder
¼ cup (2 oz.) granulated sugar
⅓ cup (1.4 oz.) nonfat milk powder
½ cup (3.3 oz.) shortening
2 eggs
1 ⅓ cups water
Frying oil or shortening

For Donut Glaze:
2 ¼ Tbs. honey
⅔ cup water
6 ½ cups confectioners' sugar

Directions:

1. Warm the yeast water to 110⁰ F in a small container and stir in the yeast.
2. Sift the cake flour and bread flour and set aside.
3. Mix the salt, baking powder, granulated sugar, milk powder, and shortening in a bowl until combined.
4. Add the eggs, one at a time, and blend.
5. Add 1 ⅓ cups of water and mix until absorbed.
6. Add the flour and yeast mixture and mix until the dough is smooth.
7. Cover the dough and let it sit for about 1 hour until doubled in size.
8. Pull up the sides of the dough, fold the sides over the center, and using your fist, press down.
9. Turn the dough upside down in the bowl.
10. On a lightly floured surface, roll out the dough ½ inch thick.
11. Cut out the donuts, using a 3 ½-inch donut cutter, and place the dough onto a lightly greased baking sheet.
12. Cover the donuts with a towel as you prepare the frying oil.
13. Clip a fat thermometer to the side of the large, high-sided skillet or fryer.
14. Heat the oil or shortening in the skillet until it reaches 375⁰ F. Keep a close watch on the temperature of the oil and adjust heat up or down to maintain 375⁰ F.

15. Add 2 to 3 donuts to the heated oil. Cook the donuts for a minute or until the bottoms are golden brown. Turn the donuts and cook the other sides about another minute.
16. Place the cooked donuts on a baking sheet lined with paper towels.
17. Let the donuts cool.

Mixing Donut Glaze:
1. Heat the water and honey to 150⁰ F.
2. Add the confectioners' sugar and mix until smooth.

3. Dip the donuts in the warm donut glaze and place on screens until the glaze is set.

Or

Ice the cooled donuts with Chocolate Icing *(see page 53)*;

Or

Roll the cooled donuts in confectioners' sugar that has been sifted with cornstarch. (Use ¼ cup of cornstarch per 1 ⅛ cup of sugar.)

SUMMER SEASON

Buck and Louise catering a wedding reception
at the Lancaster Country Club

THE SUMMER SEASON

Summer Weddings

The summer was and still is the season for brides. In the early 1960s, Uncle D.B. decided the family should venture into the lucrative wedding market. The bakery was already providing wedding cakes with an assortment of bride and groom toppers. So, my enterprising uncle bought round and rectangular folding tables, silver candelabras, silver trays, silver punch bowls, glass plates, and glass punch cups. He shopped for satin and lace and made tablecloths that were draped with bows to match the brides' colors. He partnered with Blimp Gladden, the local florist, to provide centerpieces for the tables. Uncle D.B. just saw a niche and filled it. After my grandfather, he was the second most successful entrepreneur in the family!

Most weekends in June, July, and August, my uncle catered one to three wedding receptions. For family members and employees, the weekdays beforehand were filled with washing and boxing cups, plates, and tablecloths; polishing silver; baking wedding cakes, colorful Pullman loaf bread, bite-sized pastry shells, and cheese wafers; and making chicken salad, citrus punch, and mints. (Actually, the mints were made by our cousin Annie Plyer and decorated by my father. Many may remember Annie as the lunchroom manager at McDonald Green School for twenty-three years.) Uncle D.B. also offered the brides large California strawberries for dipping in confectioners' sugar; assorted melons scooped and arranged in sculpted watermelon rinds; and Tea Ball cookies iced in the bride's colors.

Within a couple of years, my uncle was catering receptions in backyards, country clubs, and church fellowship halls in the surrounding towns. For our family, the outdoor receptions presented the most stressful work. On many occasions we had to tear down the setup and move everything indoors because of those rain showers that occur so frequently during Lancaster summers. Besides, transporting the stacked three- and four-layer wedding cakes in vans with no air conditioning was a risky endeavor. Several times the icing would soften, and the layers would tilt. Later we packed layers separately and assembled the cakes with dividers on-site. Less stress for us and a happier occasion for the bride and groom!

Bakery exhibit at the Lancaster Armory in 1955

One summer while working at the bakery during our school break, my brother Donald met a beautiful young lady, Catherine Lisenby, whom my grandfather had hired as a part-time salesclerk. Drinking Sundrops or RC colas and leaning against the drink machine, he enjoyed watching Catherine at work. Donald must have made a good impression because he and Catherine began dating. They later married on July 26, 1964, and naturally the Lancaster Bakery catered their wedding reception. In 2020, Donald and Catherine celebrated their fifty-sixth anniversary. They now live in Monroe, North Carolina, and have one son, Grant; a daughter, Stephanie; a granddaughter, Madison; and a grandson, Donald.

Buck baked and delivered a wedding cake to Jacksonville, Florida, for his niece's wedding.

WEDDING RECIPES

Tea Ball Cookies

Yield: Approximately 4 dozen cookies.

Ingredients:

For Cookies:
4 ¼ cups (20 oz.) bread flour
1 ¼ cups (8 oz.) granulated sugar
1 ¼ cups (8 oz.) shortening
1 cup (8 oz.) margarine
⅛ tsp. salt
¾ cup (3 oz.) pecans, finely chopped
1 tsp. vanilla extract
3 or 4 drops of maple flavor
*Optional flavoring: Substitute 1 tsp.
of McCormick's Vanilla, Butter & Nut
flavor for the vanilla and maple.*

For Icing:
7 ½ cups (32 oz.) confectioners' sugar
Water (variable)
Food coloring

Directions:

1. Mix all ingredients together lightly, just enough for the dough to hold together.
2. Shape 2 tsp. of the dough into a ball.
3. Place the dough 2 inches apart on a parchment-lined baking sheet.
4. Using your thumb or the back of a half-teaspoon measuring spoon, make a deep indentation in the middle of each cookie. (If the dough cracks on the sides, use your fingers to reshape.)
5. Place the baking sheet in the refrigerator for 20–30 minutes to help prevent spreading while baking.

6. Place the baking sheet in a 350⁰ F preheated oven for 20–25 minutes until the edges and bottoms of the cookies are lightly golden brown.

Mixing Icing:

1. Slowly add lukewarm water to the confectioners' sugar while stirring until the icing is smooth and is the desired consistency. (Do not make icing too stiff because it will become hard and brittle when cooled.)
2. Stir in the food coloring in the desired color.
3. Fill the indentations on top of the cooled cookies and allow an hour for the icing to set.
4. If multiple colors of icing are desired, place confectioners' sugar and water in small bowls and add food coloring as desired.

Party Punch

Yield: Approximately 2 ½ gallons of punch.

Ingredients:

¼ cup (2 oz.) citric acid
2 quarts of water
1 can frozen orange juice concentrate
  (12 oz.)
1 can pineapple juice (46 oz.)
6 ¾ cups (48 oz.) of granulated sugar
5 quarts of water

Directions:

1. Stir the citric acid in 2 quarts of the water until dissolved.
2. Add the remaining ingredients and stir until combined.

Cheese Wafers

Yield: Approximately 2 dozen cheese wafers.

Ingredients:

1 ⅔ cups (8 oz.) bread flour
1 ⅔ cups (8 oz.) cake flour
½ cup (2.3 oz.) nonfat milk powder
1 tsp. salt
2 ¾ cups (11 oz.) grated sharp
  cheddar cheese
½ cup (4 oz.) shortening
1 cup (8 oz.) margarine
Optional flavoring: Add a dash of cheddar cheese powder for flavor and color.

Directions:

1. Sift the bread flour, cake flour, milk powder, and salt.
2. Add the remaining ingredients and mix together until the dough forms.
3. Using a pastry bag fitted with a 1 M (½-inch) star tube, deposit quarter-size dough 2 inches apart on a parchment-lined baking sheet.
4. Place the baking sheet in preheated 350⁰ F oven for about 10–15 minutes.

Pound Cake

Buck used this recipe to make wedding cakes. He also used this recipe to make Petit Fours.

Ingredients:

2 ¼ cups (16 oz.) granulated sugar
1 ¼ cups (8.7 oz.) shortening
5 eggs
2 tsp. vanilla extract
1 tsp. lemon extract
2 ¾ cups (13.3 oz.) cake flour
1 ½ tsp. salt
½ Tbs. (.25 oz.) baking powder
3 Tbs. (.83 oz.) nonfat milk powder
¾ cup water

Directions:

1. Grease the pan(s) and dust with flour. *(See the pan size options below.)*
2. Have all ingredients at room temperature.
3. Cream the granulated sugar and shortening until light in color.
4. Add the eggs, one at a time, slowly, and cream together lightly. (Scrape down the sides of the mixing bowl.)
5. Blend in the vanilla extract and lemon extract.
6. Sift the cake flour, salt, baking powder, and powdered milk.
7. Alternate adding the flour mixture and the water to the creamed mixture, beginning with flour and ending with flour.

8. Pour the batter into 3 prepared loaf pans (2 ¼ inches x 3 ½ inches x 8 inches).
9. Bake at 350⁰ F for 50–60 minutes.

Or

1. Pour batter into 3 prepared 8-inch round pans.
2. Bake at 375⁰ F for 20–25 minutes.
3. Cool 15 minutes before turning the pans onto wire racks to finish cooling.

Or

1. Pour batter in a prepared sheet pan (18 inches x 13 inches).
2. Bake at 360⁰ F for 30–35 minutes.
3. Cool before cutting the cake into 1-inch by 2-inch squares (Petit Fours). Place cakes on a rack that is positioned over parchment paper. Pour the Dip Icing *(see page 85)* over the cakes. Let the icing set for about an hour.

Dip Icing

Ingredients:

⅓ cup (3 oz.) shortening
¼ cup (3 oz.) light corn syrup
9 ½ cups (40 oz.) sifted
  confectioners' sugar
Warm water, variable

*Optional: Food coloring may be added
with the ingredients if desired.*
*Optional: Add 1 tsp. clear vanilla
extract, lemon extract, or almond
extract to the ingredients.*
*Optional: 12 oz. of melted
unsweetened (bitter) chocolate can be
added for chocolate dip.*

Directions:

1. In a double boiler or a large glass bowl over a simmering pot of water, melt the shortening. (The bowl should not touch the water.)
2. Stir in the corn syrup, ½ cup warm water, and confectioners' sugar.
3. Add more warm water, a little at a time, until the icing is a smooth, thin ("soupy") consistency.
4. Remove the icing from the heat and let cool for about 3 minutes before pouring over the petit fours. If the mixture hardens prior to icing all of the cake bites, place the bowl over simmering water again to soften.
5. When cool, the icing will harden and have a smooth, glossy finish.
6. Decorate as desired.

Segregation

Segregation was practiced throughout the South before desegregation laws were passed in the mid-1960s. I, too, have memories of segregation in my hometown and other places in South Carolina. One summer during the 1950s, Mama hired a teenaged Black girl to watch over Rita and me. I don't remember her name, but I do remember she was quiet and shy. She would walk us to the public library and remain outside on the steps while my sister and I checked out books for summer reading. I told her to come in with us, but she said Black people weren't allowed in the library. One day when we were walking home under the hot sun, I sipped cool water from the public water fountain and noticed she did not drink any. Again, she said Black people weren't allowed to drink from public water fountains. Then I started noticing similar situations: The Black employees in the bakery had their own restroom; Black theater-goers sat in the movie theater balcony; Black children attended their own public schools; and Black families lived in their own section of Lancaster. Too young to understand the laws, I accepted them and only later realized I had grown up in a community that had fostered segregation for generations.

Many families, especially those with working parents, had Black maids. As youngsters, Rita and I often rode with our father to drive our maid Ola home. One summer afternoon when we were riding along, Rita said, "Daddy, you should marry Ola because you both have dark skin." Suddenly there was an awkward silence in the car. Daddy turned around and gave Rita the "evil eye." Ola didn't say a word, but I remember seeing the slightest smile crinkle the corner of her mouth. When we returned home, Daddy gave Rita a spanking she wouldn't soon forget. At the time I didn't understand why Rita was spanked.

Most summers, Uncle D.B. took Rita and me to Myrtle Beach for a week, where he rented a room in Mrs. Holden's beach-front home. We spent days lounging on the beach under the hot sun and nights riding the rides at the downtown Pavilion Amusement Park or watching movies in the air-conditioned movie theater. I clearly recall when Rita and I learned one of our first lessons about skin color. Since we had inherited our father's olive complexion, our skin turned dark, dark brown after a couple of sun-drenched days. One night at the amusement park, we ran into two girlfriends from our Lancaster neighborhood. As we approached them, they burst out laughing. Our friends claimed that when they first saw us, they thought we were Black girls. They had wondered why we were admitted to the Whites-only park. Even back at home, our skin color created problems. On several occasions, Rita and I were denied admittance to the Lancaster city pool because of our tanned skin. In hindsight, our experiences seem trivial compared to the discrimination that minorities often face daily.

Lancaster Schools were integrated in the mid-1960s, and several school activities were affected. During my junior and senior high school years, we did not have our traditional proms because the school administrators were too fearful of a confrontation between White and Black students. Thankfully, overall Lancaster Schools' integration went smoothly.

More Memories

During the summer months, we youngsters played outdoors most of the day. In the backyard Rita and I really enjoyed a sandbox and a small cement wading pool. Some days we wandered to the nearby Wylie Street Park to play on the hot metal slide or the seesaw or the merry-go-round. Sometimes we headed up the hill to the Lancaster Youth Center, a hangout for Lancaster's teens. Behind the center was a cement basketball court, where we smaller kids liked to jump and try to get our basketballs up to the towering hoops—at least until the big kids ran us off.

Rita and I occasionally joined our grandfather when he went fishing in local ponds during the early morning hours on summer days. To prepare, we used a net to scoop up minnows from the minnow pond in our backyard. Later as we sat in Pawpaw's john boat with our fishing hooks baited, we watched the corks bob on the water and waited excitedly for them to disappear beneath the surface. For our lunch, Pawpaw usually packed small apple, cherry, and lemon meringue tarts. Rita and I were always happy whether or not we caught any fish!

One summer in the early 1950s, my grandparents visited relatives in Miami, Florida. While there, my grandmother fell in love with a beautiful parrot with green and yellow feathers and brought it back to Lancaster. She named the parrot Polly. Well, Polly had a mean streak and would not hesitate to bite off the tip of someone's finger. But she did have a talent for talking and singing and joined in our family sing-alongs. On late summer afternoons, Mama would place the birdcage on our front porch. Over and over, Polly called out "Donald" loudly until my brother came home for supper. I must not neglect to mention how much Donald wanted to kill that bird!

I feel grateful to have so many years of wonderful summers but with a few exceptions. Of course, I enjoyed going with Mama to buy groceries at Mr. Taylor's store on Tuesday mornings and watching Mama get her hair styled by Mrs. Ezzell at Milady's Beauty Salon on Thursday afternoons. Still, some days being an identical twin created problems for me. On one such day, a bored Rita stood in our front yard and tried to throw small rocks at passing cars. Naturally the annoyed neighbors telephoned my parents, but unfortunately, they identified me as the one throwing the rocks. For Rita's mischievous ways, I received numerous spankings. Being an identical twin definitely has its good and bad moments!

RECIPES

Tropical Cupcakes

Yield: Approximately 2 ½ dozen cupcakes.

Ingredients:

For Cupcakes:
1 ½ cups (11 oz.) granulated sugar
⅔ cup (4.4 oz.) shortening
8 ¾ oz. crushed pineapple
2 eggs
½ tsp. salt
¾ tsp. vanilla extract
¼ cup water
2 ¼ cups (11 oz.) cake flour
1 Tbs. (.5 oz.) baking powder
1 ¼ cups (4 oz.) shredded coconut

For Glaze:
3 oz. crushed pineapple
2 cups (9 oz.) confectioners' sugar

Directions:

1. Spray bottoms and sides of two cupcake tins with cooking spray or line with paper liners.
2. Have all ingredients at room temperature.
3. Cream the granulated sugar and shortening.
4. Add the crushed pineapple and blend in.
5. Blend in eggs, salt, and vanilla extract.
6. Add the water and blend in.
7. Sift the cake flour and baking powder and mix into the creamed mixture.

8. Mix in the coconut.
9. Fill the muffin pans about ⅔ full.
10. Tap the pans on the counter to remove air bubbles and to distribute evenly.
11. Bake in a 375⁰ F preheated oven for about 10 minutes.

Mixing Icing:
1. Stir together the crushed pineapple and confectioners' sugar.
2. Spread the glaze on top of the cooled cupcakes.

Lemon Chiffon Cake

Yield: 1 8-inch cake.

Ingredients:

For Cake:
1 ¾ cups (9 oz.) cake flour
1 ¾ cups (12.15 oz.) granulated sugar
  (divided, 1 ¼ cups and ½ cup)
⅔ Tbs. (.34 oz.) baking powder
1 tsp. salt
¼ cup (1 oz.) nonfat milk powder
⅓ cup (3.2 oz.) vegetable oil
1 ⅛ cups (9 oz.) water
3 egg yolks
¾ tsp. (.08 oz.) cream of tartar
3 egg whites
1 pkg. (7 oz.) of frozen shredded
  coconut, thawed

For Icing:
2 cups granulated sugar
½ cup lemon juice
4 eggs, slightly beaten
2 egg whites
1 Tbs. unsalted butter

Directions:
1. Preheat oven to 375⁰ F.
2. Have all ingredients at
   room temperature.
3. Grease and flour, bottom only, of
   three 8-inch round pans.
4. Sift the cake flour, 1 ¼ cups of
   granulated sugar, baking powder,
   salt, and milk powder into the
   mixing bowl.
5. Add the vegetable oil, water,
   and egg yolks to the sifted dry
   ingredients and mix on medium
   speed until smooth (about
   2–3 minutes).
6. In a separate mixing bowl, add the
   cream of tartar to the egg whites
   and whip to a light peak. Then
   gradually add ½ cup of granulated
   sugar and continue whipping until
   the mixture is very stiff and glossy.
7. Fold the whipped egg whites into
   the flour mixture.
8. Immediately pour the batter into
   the prepared pans.
9. Place the pans in the preheated
   oven, and bake the cake
   approximately 20 minutes.
10. After baking, immediately turn
    pans upside down on a rack and
    allow the cake to cool before
    loosening from pans.
11. Brush excess crumbs from the
    cooled cake layers. Place the
    bottom layer, flat side up, on a cake
    board or platter.
12. Spread a thin layer of the
    cooled icing on top of the layer
    to the edges.
13. Sprinkle thawed coconut on top of
    the icing.

14. Place the middle layer over the bottom layer, and spread a thin layer of icing on the top to the edges.
15. Place the top layer over the middle layer, rounded side up.
16. Using a spatula, place a thin layer of icing on center of the top layer and spread to the edges and down the sides of the cake.
17. Press thawed coconut on the top and sides of cake.

Mixing Icing:
1. Place the sugar and lemon juice in a saucepan.
2. Add the eggs and egg whites and whisk together quickly.
3. Cook over medium heat, whisking the mixture until it comes to a boil and thickens.
4. Remove the mixture from the stove and stir in the butter until it is melted and thoroughly blended.

Mediterranean Macaroon Cookies

Yield: Approximately 5 dozen cookies.

Ingredients:

4 ¾ cups (20 oz.) confectioners' sugar
3 cups (10 oz.) macaroon coconut
1 ⅛ cups (6 oz.) chopped dates
½ cup (4 oz.) granulated sugar
6 egg whites
½ tsp. salt
1 cup (4 oz.) ground pecans

Directions:

1. Preheat oven to 380^0 F.
2. Mix all ingredients on medium speed for 2 minutes until smooth.
3. Drop the cookies by teaspoon 2 inches apart on a parchment-lined baking sheet.
4. Place the baking sheet in the oven and bake the cookies for approximately 10–12 minutes or until lightly browned.
5. Move the baking sheet to a wire rack to cool for 10 minutes. Slide the parchment onto a wire rack to finish cooling.

Angel Food Cake

Yield: 1 10-inch cake.

Ingredients:

19 egg whites
2 ⅔ cups (19.1 oz.) granulated sugar
  (divided 1 ⅓ cups and 1 ⅓ cups)
1 ⅓ tsp. salt
2 ¾ tsp. (.30 oz.) cream of tartar
1 tsp. vanilla extract
1 ¼ cups (6 oz.) cake flour

Directions:

1. Preheat oven to 350⁰ F.
2. Have all ingredients at room temperature.
3. Whip the egg whites until they form a light peak.
4. Sift 1 ⅓ cups of granulated sugar, salt, and the cream of tartar.
5. Add the sugar mixture to the egg whites along with the vanilla extract, and continue to whip to bring eggs to a medium peak.
6. Sift the cake flour and the remaining 1 ⅓ cups of granulated sugar three times. Add to the above mixture on low speed and stop the mixer as soon as the flour mixture is incorporated.
7. Pour the batter into an ungreased 10-inch tube pan and bake immediately for 50 minutes.
8. Turn the pan upside down on a rack and allow the cake to cool. Use a spatula to loosen the sides of cake from the pan when cooled.

EPILOGUE

Tragically for my family and me, my life as a twin ended after lunch on a hot August day in 1964. Rita was fifteen. During lunch that day, Rita had asked my mother if she could go back to school. Mama said that wasn't possible because Rita was several years behind her classmates academically. In addition, the traditional six-period school day would be a challenge for someone who has several epileptic seizures a day. Then Rita left the room, locked herself in my parents' bedroom, and shot herself in the forehead with Daddy's pistol. When Daddy came home from work around 1:30 p.m., he broke into the bedroom and found my sister lying in a pool of blood. I was directly behind him. For the next week, the Lancaster Bakery was closed for mourning. The mourning has continued much longer for our family.

In the days following Rita's death, Lancaster citizens visited our house to offer their condolences. The kitchen table, countertops, and dining room table were overflowing with food that relatives and friends provided, but the family had no appetite. The days and nights were a blur, each of us lost in our own memories, trying to make sense out of what had happened and how it could have been prevented.

I remembered elementary school days. Rita and I were identical twins, wearing identical clothes, attending the same classrooms with the same teachers. Although my parents and the school administrators meant well, their actions stifled the self-identity that Rita and I needed.

During our pre-adolescent years, our paths began to diverge, and there was a growing conflict and resentment between us. I wasn't allowed to take swimming lessons or dance lessons or join the Brownies and Girl Scouts because Rita was barred from these activities because of the stigma associated with epilepsy. As I was widening my social circle, I spent much of my free time at friends' homes. Though Rita became friends with two neighborhood girls, she wasn't allowed sleepovers or long visits because of her seizures.

Our adolescent and teen years brought an end to Rita's formal education because the middle and high schools offered no services or programs to educate youths afflicted with epilepsy. So, Rita began working from 4:30 a.m. to 11:30 a.m. at the Lancaster Bakery. For six days a week, she filled phone orders, wrapped breads, and moved the confections from the production area to the retail area. The bakery employees became her extended family. All of them grieved as we did when she died, and all attended her funeral.

Several years of counseling helped me to come to terms with my grief and feelings of guilt. Could I have shown Rita more love and compassion? Could I have included her in excursions with my girlfriends? Finally, I am at peace with myself. I can even smile as I imagine Rita also at peace, playing her accordion for Mawmaw, Pawpaw, Uncle D.B., Mama, and Daddy.

***

There are 3.4 million people with epilepsy in the U.S. and about 65 million globally. The Epilepsy Foundation (www.Epilepsy.com) accepts donations to invest in epilepsy research, to train people in seizure recognition and first aid, and to assist families through its 24/7 Helpline. To do my part to make a difference, I am committing ten percent of my book royalties to the Epilepsy Foundation.

ACKNOWLEDGMENTS

The real credit belongs to my family and to all of the employees of the Lancaster Bakery.

My thanks go to the following contributors:
- My brother Donald (Ernie) Hinson and his wife Catherine for validating my early childhood memories.
- My gifted editor and friend, Sheryl Tharpe, and her talented husband, Coleman, who provided copies of photos suitable for publishing.
- Photographer Travis Bell, who granted me permission to use the Lancaster Bakery photos contained in The Lancaster Archive Web site (www.lancasterarchive.com).
- Wayne Carter and Nancy Kirk for testing some of the recipes and providing valuable feedback.
- My Warren Publishing Team (Mindy Kuhn, Amy Ashby, and Monika Dziamka) for their professionalism, guidance, and patience.
- Most important, the Lancaster Bakery's cherished customers, who provided their memories.

RECIPE INDEX BY SEASONS

A

F

W

S

AUTHOR'S BIO

Anita Hinson Cauthen grew up in the small, Southern textile town of Lancaster, South Carolina. Her youth, full of joy and celebrations and tears, centered on her extended family of eight and the family business, the Lancaster Bakery. In the early 1980s, Anita moved to nearby Rock Hill, South Carolina, to marry, raise a family, and complete her college education. She received a B.S. degree in Business and Information Management from Winthrop University in Rock Hill in 1984.

For thirty years, Anita worked in Information Management and Project Management for an insurance company and an energy company in Charlotte, North Carolina. She is a proud mother of her sons—Robert, William, and John—and her grandchildren—Brooke, Courtney, and Ethan. Anita is enjoying retirement in Rock Hill with her loving companion, a Pekingese named Nash, and she continues to write stories about her coming of age in Lancaster.